Purgatory

Devotions and How to Avoid Purgatory

My Jesus,
By the sorrows You suffered
In Your agony in the garden,
In the scourging and crowning with thorns,
In the way to Calvary,
In Your Crucifixion and Death,
Have mercy on the souls in Purgatory,
Especially those who are most forsaken,
Deliver them from the dire torments they
endure, and admit them to Your most sweet
embrace in paradise.
Our Father, Hail Mary, Glory Be
Eternal Rest grant unto them, O Lord,
And let the perpetual light shine upon them.
May they rest in peace.
Amen.

Table of Contents

- Introduction 4
- Meditation: The Key to Avoiding Purgatory..................5
- What Is Purgatory?...8
- Our Duty to the Poor Souls...10
  - Saint Alphonsus on Our Duty to the Poor Souls............10
  - Read Me or Rue It...14
    - Forward 14
    - What is Purgatory?...15
    - Can all this be true?...17
    - How long do souls remain in Purgatory?...................19
    - Why pray for the poor souls?..23
    - How can we help the Holy Souls?................................27
    - What the Holy Souls do for those who help them......29
  - How To Grieve For Your Dead..38
    - Two Very Special Points..38
    - Motives Mortified Into Joy...39
    - Deeds of Mercy for the Dead...41
    - Valuable Reminders...42
    - Harmful Attitudes...44
- How To Avoid Purgatory...47
  - Resignation to the Death God Wills for Us....................48
    - Trustful Surrender to Divine Providence..................48
    - From Saint Alphonsus...48
    - Recapitulation..49
  - The Desire For Heaven 50
  - Purge All Attachments to the World..............................51
  - Detest All of Our Sins, Mortal and Venial.....................53
  - How to Gain a Plenary Indulgence..................................54
  - How to Avoid Purgatory..55
    - Can We Avoid Purgatory? Yes. 55
    - How Can We Avoid Purgatory?....................................55
    - The First Means: Removing the Cause......................56
    - The Second Means: Penance...57
    - The Third Means: Suffering..58
    - The Fourth Means: Confession, Communion, Holy Mass...........59
    - The Fifth Means: Asking God..60
    - A Sixth Means: Resignation to Death........................61

- The Seventh Means: Extreme Unction.................................61
- Indulgences and Purgatory..62
- The Third Orders..63
- Those Who Earnestly Help the Holy Souls May Well Hope to Avoid Purgatory..64
- To Avoid Purgatory, Do As Follows....................................65
- Form of Oblation..69

Devotions For the Relief of the Poor Suffering Souls in Purgatory.....70
- Office of the Dead 71
  - Matins...71
  - Lauds of the Dead...87
  - Vespers of the Dead..94
  - Special Prayers For the Dead......................................99
- Daily Pilgrimage to Purgatory 105
  - Origin Of The Daily Pilgrimage To Purgatory 105
  - The Daily Pilgrimage To Purgatory............................107
  - A Pious Union of Prayer 107
- Prayers for the Daily Pilgrimage to Purgatory 110
  - Sunday 111
  - Monday 113
  - Tuesday 114
  - Wednesday 115
  - Thursday 117
  - Friday 118
  - Saturday 120
- Novena For The Relief Of The Poor Souls In Purgatory..............122
  - Preparatory Prayer..123
  - De Profundis (Psalm 129) 124
  - First Day: Existence of Purgatory 125
  - Second Day: Pains of Purgatory 126
  - Third Day: The Pain of Loss......................................127
  - Fourth Day: The Pain of Sense 129
  - The Fifth Day: Duration of Purgatory 130
  - The Sixth Day: Obligation of Assisting the "Poor Souls." 132
  - The Seventh Day: Cruelty of Those Who Abandon the "Poor Souls." 133
  - The Eighth Day: The Communion of Saints 135
  - The Ninth Day: Benefit of the Devotion to the "Poor Souls." . 136

Introduction

The duty we have to pray for other people, living and dead, cannot be overemphasized. We have a duty in justice to pray for our family members, living or dead; our parents, our grand parents; our brothers and sisters; our children, etc. We have a duty to pray for our pastors, past and present, our Bishop and the Pope. We have a duty to pray for our employer, our friends and neighbors and all we do business with. We even have a duty to pray for our enemies.

Unfortunately, when people die, they are soon forgotten and left to languish unaided in Purgatory. This book is dedicated to aiding all in Purgatory.

This book will serve three purposes. The first purpose is to help us become saints, for saints can release far more souls than sinners can. To this end we have reproduced <u>How to Avoid Pugatory</u> with an important addition. Saint John Massias released 1,400,000 souls! Before that section is the section on our duty to the poor souls in Purgatory. This contains <u>Read Me or Rue It</u> and other useful advice. We conclude with many devotions for the Poor Souls. The Office of the Dead is said by the clergy as part of their duty in the burial of the dead in their parishes. It is recommended to begin the <u>The Novena for the Relief of the Poor Souls</u> for a person the day he or she dies. And Saint Margaret Mary recommends making a <u>Daily Pilgrimage to Purgatory</u> every night. What an excellent addition to our night prayers!

We pray that this book will help you become a Saint and also help many be released from the tortures and prison of Purgatory!

Brother Hermenegild

Meditation: The Key to Avoiding Purgatory

Although we intend on covering our duty to the Poor Souls first, there is one key to avoiding Purgatory that must come before all else. In fact, this alone could help us become great saints, if only we are faithful to this one practice daily until the end of our lives. This practice is meditation. All of the saints and spiritual authors tell us that if we take up meditation and remain faithful, we will give up sin. Meditation, also called mental prayer, and sin cannot coexist in the soul. It therefore would be foolish not to take up this holy practice.

The Catholic's Manual tells us: "In effect, nothing more is requisite for Meditation, than to be a reasonable creature, because Meditation is nothing more than an exercise of the three powers of the soul-memory, understanding, and will; that is, an application of these three powers to some particular subject, whether spiritual or temporal. Therefore, it is clear that Meditation, rightly understood, it not only easy, but universally practiced, since all, from the highest to the lowest, have some object in view; some scheme to accomplish; some business to pursue; and there is no one, if he wish to avoid being rash or foolish, who does not frequently reflect on and adopt the means most likely to insure success. A Saint is not distinguished from a worldling, precisely by reflecting or meditating more frequently and more profoundly; but by a difference in the subject of his reflections or meditations. It is on the concerns of the soul only that Meditation is found troublesome and difficult. For example, what difficulty does a merchant find in meditating, that is, in reasoning or reflecting on commerce? A farmer on husbandy? A tradesman on his employment? Those persons frequently call to mind what they have heard and read, for or against the plans they pursue, and thus they exercise the memory. They make serious reflections upon what they have found profitable or the reverse, and consider frequently how far their plans are calculated to insure success, or expose them to failure; this is the exercise of the understanding. Lastly, however, little capacity those persons may have, their reflections never fail to excite in their will hopes and desires of success, fears of danger, or sorrow for failures; this is the exercise of the will. And these same reflections afterwards urge them to take precautions against the accidents they foresee, and adopt such measures as may repair past losses, and insure ultimate success."

We all think, so it is merely a matter of purifying what and how we think. We use our ability to reason to sanctify ourselves by thinking on holy things on a daily basis. This is all that is required.

Fr. John Henry tells us: "By insisting on the moral necessity of mental prayer, St. Alphonsus does not demand that every one must follow a certain method. There are many methods and degrees of mental prayer. There is a method of mental prayer that all can use, viz., calling to mind a sermon; reading from some pious book and stopping between the sentences; then reflecting a moment, applying the reading, etc., to oneself, making short aspirations, asking for pardon, for help of grace and taking an appropriate resolution. By this means many are converted on missions and in retreats. This sort of mental prayer may be said to be necessary for all Christians to obtain conversion and holy perseverance."

Saint Teresa used a book for eighteen years and this book can be the beginning of your spiritual life. To use this or any other book to help in meditation, take notes. In fact it is good to start a spiritual notebook and write your meditation points in there. And when you pray, don't just read the prayers, think about them. Both <u>Daily Pilgrimage to Purgatory</u> and <u>The Novena for the Relief of the Poor Souls</u> have meditations contained in them.

In the <u>Daily Pilgrimage to Purgatory</u> we meditate daily on one of the regrets of the Poor Souls on what they wish they had done differently in their life on earth. Each one of these *regrets* can teach us what we should be doing different here and now.

<u>The Novena for the Relief of the Poor Souls</u> tells us: "So the Souls in Purgatory, plaintive and doleful, long for the joys of the heavenly mansion. They have had a glimpse of its glory and happiness, but because they were too much attached to earthly pleasures, they will be deprived, perhaps for a long time, of the celestial joys." Let us meditate that today we live in an age, which is devoted to earthly pleasures. We have pleasures unheard of twenty years ago and especially a century ago. Consider the home theater. A century ago, it was difficult to get to the theater once a month, and yet a pious author reminds us that it is not to the theater that we go

to save our soul!   Consider what we can purchase easily in the grocery store, that would have been unavailable to our grand parents just a few decades ago! Saint Paul was right, when he said: "she that lives in pleasures is dead while she is alive." (I Timothy 5:6) Let us meditate whether we are spiritually dead ,because we are plugged into the world, or have we detached from the world as we pray in the third Joyful Mystery: "Let us detach from earthly things." Yes, it is time to *unplug* from the world and to *plug in* to Almighty God. And let us consider that if we have not completely detached from the world in this life, we will have to spend decades, possibly centuries, in Purgatory completing the task.

    And so we have just completed a meditation, if we have considered the above points well and applied them to our life and resolved to unplug from the world here and now, so that we can become a saint.

What Is Purgatory?

The <u>Baltimore Catechism</u> tells us: "Purgatory is the state in which those suffer for a time who die guilty of venial sins, or without having satisfied for the punishment due to their sins.

""Punishment"--that is, temporal punishment. After the general judgment there will be Heaven and Hell, but no Purgatory, for there will be no men living or dying upon the earth in its present condition to go there. All will be dead and judged and sent to their final abodes. Those in Purgatory are the friends of God; and knowing Him as they do now, they would not go into His holy presence with the slightest stain upon their souls; still they are anxious for their Purgatory to be ended that they may be with God. They suffer, we are told, the same pains of sense as the damned; but they suffer willingly, for they know that it is making them more pleasing to God, and that one day it will all be over and He will receive them into Heaven. Their salvation is sure, and that thought makes them happy. If, therefore, you believe any of your friends are in Purgatory, you should help them all you can, and try by your prayers and good works to shorten their time of suffering. They will help you--though they cannot help themselves--by their prayers. And oh, when they are admitted into Heaven, how they will pray for those that have helped them out of Purgatory! If you do this great charity, God will, when you die, put in some good person's heart to pray for you while you suffer in Purgatory. There must be a Purgatory, for one who dies with the slightest stain of sin upon his soul cannot enter Heaven, and yet God would not send him to Hell for so small a sin. But why does God punish those He loves? Why does He not forgive everything? He punishes because He is infinitely just and true. He warned them that if they did certain things they would be punished; and they did them, and God must keep His promise. Moreover He is just, and must give to everyone exactly what he deserves."

There are three states in the spiritual life for those striving for heaven. These are the purgative, the illuminitive and the unitive ways. A soul progresses from the purgative to illuminitive and then to the unitive way and then straight into heave. Those souls, which do not complete the trip will spend time in Purgatory completing the work. Notice that the purgative way sounds a lot like Purgatory. No one who has not completed the purgative way will go straight to heaven. So let us consider the purgative way.

"The purgative way is the way of beginners in the spiritual life. Their duty is to purge the soul from sin and sinful habits by the constant practice of mortification and mental prayer." (<u>Spiritual Direction</u>, Parente) The Catechism of the Council of Trent tells us that the whole life of a Christian should be a perpetual penance. And we just learned that mental prayer is the road to heaven.

Let us therefore purge ourselves here on earth of all of our sinful habits by prayer and penance, so that we can go straight to heaven. And while doing this, let us also pray for the Poor Souls in Purgatory.

Our Duty to the Poor Souls

Saint Alphonsus on Our Duty to the Poor Souls

Is it good to invoke the souls in purgatory?

Again, it is disputed whether there is any use in recommending one's self to the souls in purgatory. Some say that the souls in that state cannot pray for us; and these rely on the authority of St. Thomas, who says that those souls, while they are being purified by pain, are inferior to us, and therefore 'are not in a state to pray for us, but rather require our prayers.' But many other Doctors, as Bellarmine, Sylvius, Cardinal Gotti, Lessius, Medina and others affirm with great probability, that we should piously believe that God manifests our prayer to those holy souls in order that they may pray for us; and that so the charitable interchange of mutual prayer may be kept up between them and us. Nor do St. Thomas' words present much difficulty; for, as Sylvius and Gotti say, it is one thing not to be in a state to pray, another not to be able to pray. It is true that those souls are not in a state to pray, because, as St. Thomas says, while suffering they are inferior to us, and rather require our prayers; nevertheless, in this state they are well able to pray, as they are friends of God. If a father keeps a son whom he tenderly loves in confinement for some fault; if the son then is not in a state to pray for himself, is that any reason why he cannot pray for others? and may he not expect to obtain what he asks, knowing, as he does, his father's affection for him? So the souls in purgatory, being beloved by God, and confirmed in grace, have absolutely no impediment to prevent them from praying for us. Still the Church does not invoke them, or implore their intercession, because ordinarily they have no cognizance of our prayers. But we may piously believe that God makes our prayers known to them; and then they, full of charity as they are, most assuredly do not omit to pray for us. St. Catharine of Bologna, whenever she desired any favour, had recourse to the souls in purgatory, and was immediately heard. She even testified that by the intercession of the souls in purgatory she had obtained many graces which she had not been able to obtain by the intercession of the saints.

Our duty to pray for the souls in purgatory.

Here let me make a digression in favour of those holy souls. If we desire the aid of their prayers, it is but fair that we should mind to aid them with our prayers and good works. I said it is fair, but I should have said it is a Christian duty; for charity obliges us to succour our neighbour when he requires our aid, and we can help him without grievous inconvenience. Now it is certain that amongst our neighbours are to be reckoned the souls in purgatory, who, although no longer living in this world, yet have not left the communion of saints. 'The souls of the pious dead,' says St. Augustine, 'are not separated from the Church,' and St. Thomas says more to our purpose, that the charity which is due to the dead who died in the grace of God is only an extension of the same charity which we owe to our neighbour while living: 'Charity, which is the bond which unites the members of the Church, extends not only to the living, but also to the dead who die in charity.' Therefore, we ought to succour, according to our ability, those holy souls as our neighbours; and as their necessities are greater than those of our other neighbours, our duty to succour them seems also to be greater.

But now, what are the necessities of those holy prisoners? It is certain that their pains are immense. The fire that tortures them, says St. Augustine, is more excruciating than any pain that man can endure in this life: That fire will be more painful than anything that man can suffer in this life.' St. Thomas thinks the same, and supposes it to be identical with the fire of hell: 'The damned are tormented and the elect purified in the same fire.' And this only relates to the pains of sense. But the pain of loss (that is, the privation of the sight of God), which those holy souls suffer, is much greater; because not only their natural affection, but also the supernatural love of God, wherewith they burn, draws them with such violence to be united with their Sovereign Good, that when they see the barrier which their sins have put in the way, they feel a pain so acute, that if they were capable of death, they could not live a moment. So that, as St. Chrysostom says, this pain of the deprivation of God tortures them incomparably more than the pain of sense: 'The flames of a thousand hells together could not inflict such torments as the pain of loss by itself.' So that those holy souls would rather suffer every other possible torture than be deprived for a single instant of the union with God for which they long. So St. Thomas says that the pain of purgatory exceeds anything that can be endured in this life: 'The pain of purgatory must exceed all pain of this life.' And Dionysius the Carthusian relates, that a dead person, who had been raised to life by the intercession of St. Jerome, told St. Cyril of Jerusalem that all the torments of this earth are refreshing and delightful when compared with the very least pain of purgatory: If all the torments of the world were compared with the least that can be had in purgatory they would appear comfortable.' And he adds, that if a man had once tried those torments, he would rather suffer all the earthly sorrows that man can endure till the Day of Judgment, than suffer for one day the least pain of purgatory. Hence St. Cyril wrote to St. Augustine: 'That as far as regards the infliction of suffering, these pains are the same as those of hell -- their only difference being that they are not eternal.' Hence we see that the pains of these holy souls are excessive, while, on the other hand, they cannot help themselves; because as Job says: They are in chains and are bound with the cords of poverty (Job 36, 8). They are destined to reign with Christ; but they are withheld from taking possession of their kingdom till the time of their purgation is accomplished. And they cannot help themselves (at least not sufficiently, even according to those theologians who assert that they can by their prayers gain some relief,) to throw off their chains, until they have entirely satisfied the justice of God. This is precisely what a Cistercian monk said to the sacristan of his monastery: 'Help me, I beseech you, with your prayers; for of myself I can obtain nothing.' And this is consistent with the saying of St. Bonaventure: 'Destitution prevents solvency.' That is, those souls are so poor, that they have no means of making satisfaction.

On the other hand, since it is certain, and even of faith, that by our suffrages, and chiefly by our prayers, as particularly recommended and practiced by the Church, we can relieve those holy souls, I do not know how to excuse that man from sin who neglects to give them some assistance, at least by his prayers. If a sense of duty will not persuade us to succour them, let us think of the pleasure it will give Jesus Christ to see us endeavouring to deliver his beloved spouses from prison, in order that he may have them with him in paradise. Let us think of the store of merit which we can lay up by practicing this great act of charity; let us think, too, that those souls are not ungrateful, and will never forget the great benefit we do them in relieving them of their pains, and in obtaining for them, by our prayers, anticipation of their entrance into glory; so that when they are there they will never neglect to pray for us. And if God promises mercy to him who practices mercy towards his neighbour -- Blessed are the merciful for they shall obtain mercy (Mt. 5, 7) -- he may reasonably expect to be saved who remembers to assist those souls so afflicted, and yet so dear to God. Jonathan, after having saved the Hebrews from ruin by a victory over their enemies, was condemned to death by his father Saul for having tasted some honey against his express commands; but the people came before the king, and said, Shall Jonathan then die, who hath wrought this great salvation in Israel? (I Samuel 14,45). So may we expect that if any of us ever obtains, by his prayers, the liberation of a soul from purgatory, that soul will say to God: 'Lord, suffer not him who has delivered me from my torments to be lost.' And if Saul spared Jonathan's life at the request of his people, God will not refuse the salvation of a Christian to the prayers of a soul which is his own spouse. Moreover, St. Augustine says that God will cause those who in this life have most succoured those holy souls, when they come to purgatory themselves, to be most succoured by others. l may here observe that, in practice, one of the best suffrages is to hear Mass for them, and during the Holy Sacrifice to recommend them to God by the merits and passion of Jesus Christ. The following form may be used: 'Eternal Father, I offer you this Sacrifice of the Body and Blood of Jesus Christ, with all the pains which he suffered in his life and death; and by his passion I recommend to you the souls in purgatory, and especially that of...'etc. And it is a very charitable act to recommend, at the same time, the souls of all those who are at the point of death.

Read Me or Rue It

APPROVAL OF HIS EMINENCE THE CARDINAL PATRIARCH OF LISBON

Cardinal's Palace, Lisbon March 4, 1936

We approve and recommend with all our heart the beautiful little book Read Me or Rue It by E. D. M.

Although small, it is destined to do great good among Catholics, many of whom are incredibly ignorant of the great doctrine of Purgatory. As a consequence, they do little or nothing to avoid it themselves and little to help the Poor Souls who are suffering there so intensely, waiting for the Masses and prayers, which should be offered for them.

It is our earnest desire that every Catholic should read this little book and spread it about as widely as possible.

Read Me or Rue It

Forward
"READ ME OR RUE IT"

This title is somewhat startling. Yet, Dear Reader, if you peruse this little book, you will see for yourself how well deserved it is. The book tells us how to save ourselves and how to save others from untold suffering. Some books are good and may be read with profit. Others are better and should be read without fail.

There are, however, books of such sterling worth by reason of the counsels they suggest, the conviction they carry with them, the urge to action they give us that it would be sheer folly not to read them.

Read Me or Rue It belongs to this class. It is for your best interest, Dear Friend, to read it and reread it, to ponder well and deeply on its contents. You will never regret it; rather, great and poignant will be your regret if you fail to study its few but pregnant pages.

PURGATORY

"Have pity on me, have pity on me, at least you my friends, because the hand of the Lord hath touched me. " (Job 19:21).

This is the touching prayer that the Poor Souls in Purgatory address to their friends on Earth, begging, imploring their help, in accents of the deepest anguish. Alas, many are deaf to their prayers!

It is incomprehensible how some Catholics, even those who are otherwise devout, shamefully neglect the souls in Purgatory. It would almost seem that they do not believe in Purgatory. Certain it is that their ideas on the subject are very hazy.

Days and weeks and months pass without their having a Mass said for the Holy Souls! Seldom, too, do they hear Mass for them, seldom do they pray for them, seldom do they think of them! Whilst they are enjoying the fullness of health and happiness, busy with their work, engrossed with their amusements, the Poor Souls are suffering unutterable agonies on their beds of flame. What is the cause of this awful callousness? Ignorance: gross, inexplicable ignorance.

People do not realize what Purgatory is. They have no conception of its dreadful pains, and they have no idea of the long years that souls are detained in these awful fires. As a result, they take little or no care to avoid Purgatory themselves, and worse still, they cruelly neglect the Poor Souls who are already there and who depend entirely on them for help.

Dear Reader, peruse this little book with care and you will bless the day that it fell into your hands.

What is Purgatory?

It is a prison of fire in which nearly all [saved] souls are plunged after death and in which they suffer the intensest pain.

Here is what the great Doctors of the Church tell us of Purgatory: So grievous is their suffering that one minute in this awful fire seems like a century.

St. Thomas Aquinas, the Prince of Theologians, says that the fire of Purgatory is equal in intensity to the fire of Hell, and that the slightest contact with it is more dreadful than all the possible sufferings of this Earth!

St. Augustine, the greatest of the Holy Doctors, teaches that to be purified of their faults previous to being admitted to Heaven, souls after death are subjected to a fire more penetrating, more dreadful than anything we can see, or feel, or conceive in this life.

"Though this fire is destined to cleanse and purify the soul," adds the Holy Doctor, "still it is more acute than anything we could possibly endure on Earth. "

St. Cyril of Alexandria does not hesitate to say that "it would be preferable to suffer all the possible torments of Earth until the Judgment day than to pass one day in Purgatory. "

Another great Saint says: "Our fire, in comparison with the fire of Purgatory, is as a refreshing breeze. "

The other holy writers speak in identical terms of this awful fire.

How Comes It That the Pains of Purgatory Are So Severe?

The fire we see on Earth was made by the goodness of God for our comfort and well-being. Still, when used as a torment, it is the most dreadful one we can imagine.

The fire of Purgatory, on the contrary, was made by the Justice of God to punish and purify us and is, therefore, incomparably more severe.

Our fire, at most, burns this gross body of ours, made of clay; whereas, the fire of Purgatory acts on the spiritual soul, which is unspeakably more sensitive to pain.

The more intense our fire is, the more speedily it destroys its victim, who therefore ceases to suffer; whereas, the fire of Purgatory inflicts the keenest, most violent pain, but never kills the soul nor lessens its sensibility.

Unsurpassingly severe as is the fire of Purgatory, the pain of loss or separation from God, which the souls also suffer in Purgatory, is far more severe. The soul separated from the body craves with all the intensity of its spiritual nature for God. It is consumed with an intense desire to fly to Him. Yet it is held back. No words can describe the anguish of this unsatisfied craving.

What madness, therefore, it is for intelligent beings to neglect taking every possible precaution to avoid such a dreadful fate.

It is puerile to say that it cannot be so, that we cannot understand it, that it is better not to think or speak of it. The fact remains always the same -- whether we believe it, or whether we do not -- that the pains of Purgatory are beyond everything we can imagine or conceive. These are the words of St. Augustine.

Can all this be true?

The existence of Purgatory is so certain that no Catholic has ever entertained a doubt of it. It was taught from the earliest days of the Church and was accepted with undoubting faith wherever the Gospel was preached.

The doctrine is revealed in Holy Scripture and has been handed down by Tradition, taught by the infallible Church and believed by the millions and millions of faithful of all times.

Yet, as we have remarked, the ideas of many are vague and superficial on this most important subject They are like a person who closes his eyes and walks deliberately over the edge of a yawning precipice.

They would do well to remember that the best means of lessening our term in Purgatory -- or of avoiding it altogether -- is to have clear ideas of it, to think well on it and to adopt the means God offers for avoiding it.

Not to think of it is fatal. It is nothing else than preparing for themselves a fearfully long and rigorous Purgatory.

The Polish Prince

A Polish prince who, for some political reason, had been exiled from his native country bought a beautiful castle and property in France.

Unfortunately, he had lost the Faith of his childhood and was at the time of our story engaged in writing a book against God and the existence of a future life.

Strolling one evening in his garden, he came upon a poor woman weeping bitterly. He questioned her as to the cause of her grief.

"Ah! Prince," she replied, "I am the wife of Jean [John] Marie, your former steward, who died two days ago. He was a good husband to me and a faithful servant to Your Highness. His sickness was long and I spent all our savings on the doctors, and now I have nothing left to get Masses said for his soul. "

The Prince, touched by her grief, said a few kind words and, though professing no longer to believe in a future life, gave her some gold coins to have Masses said for her husband's soul.

Some time after, it was again evening, and the Prince was in his study working feverishly at his book.

He heard a loud rap at the door and without looking up called out to the visitor to come in. The door slowly opened and a man entered and stood facing the Prince's writing table.

On glancing up, what was not the Prince's amazement to see Jean Marie, his dead steward, looking at him with a sweet smile.

"Prince," he said, "I come to thank you for the Masses you enabled my wife to have said for my soul. Thanks to the saving Blood of Christ, which was offered for me, I am now going to Heaven, but God has allowed me to come and thank you for your generous alms. "

He then added impressively: "Prince, there is a God, a future life, a Heaven and a Hell. "

Having said these words he disappeared.

The Prince fell upon his knees and poured forth a fervent Credo.

St. Antoninus And His Friend

Here is a narrative of a different kind, but not less instructive.

St. Antoninus, the illustrious Archbishop of Florence, relates that a pious gentleman had died, who was a great friend of the Dominican Convent in which the Saint resided. Many Masses and suffrages were offered for his soul.

The Saint was very much afflicted when, after the lapse of a long time, the soul of the poor gentleman appeared to him, suffering excruciating pains.

"Oh, my Dear Friend," exclaimed the Archbishop, "are you still in Purgatory, you who led such a pious and devout life?"

"Yes, and I shall remain there still for a long time, "replied the poor sufferer, "for when on Earth I neglected to offer suffrages for the souls in Purgatory. Now, God by a just judgment has applied the suffrages which have been offered for me to those souls for whom I should have prayed. "

"But God, too, in His Justice, will give me all the merits of my good works when I enter Heaven; but first of all, I have to expiate my grave neglect in regard to others. "

So true are the words of Our Lord: "By that measure with which you measure, it will be measured to you again. "

Remember, you who read these lines, that the terrible fate of this pious gentleman will be the fate of all those who neglect to pray for and refuse to help the Holy Souls.

How long do souls remain in Purgatory?

The length of time souls are detained in Purgatory depends on: the number of their faults; the malice and deliberation with which these have been committed; the penance done, or not done, the satisfaction made, or not made for sins during life;

Much, too, depends on the suffrages offered for them after death.

What can safely be said is that the time souls spend in Purgatory is, as a rule, very much longer than people commonly imagine. We will quote a few of the many instances which are recounted in the lives and revelations of the Saints.

St. Louis Bertrand's father was an exemplary Christian, as we should naturally expect, being the father of so great a Saint. He had even wished to become a Carthusian monk until he learned that it was not God's will for him.

When he died, after long years spent in the practice of every Christian virtue, his saintly son, fully aware of the rigors of God's

Justice, offered many Masses and poured forth the most fervent supplications for the soul he so dearly loved.

A vision of his father still in Purgatory forced him to intensify a hundredfold his suffrages. He added most severe penances and long fasts to his Masses and prayers. Yet eight whole years passed before he obtained the release of his father.

St. Malachy's sister was detained in Purgatory for a very long time, despite the Masses, prayers and heroic mortifications the Saint offered for her!

It was related to a holy nun in Pampluna, who had succeeded in releasing many Carmelite nuns from Purgatory, that most of these had spent there terms of from 30 to 60 years!

Carmelite nuns in Purgatory for 40, 50 and 60 years! What will it be for those living amidst the temptations of the World and with all their hundreds of weaknesses?

St. Vincent Ferrer, after the death of his sister, prayed with incredible fervor for her soul and offered many Masses for her release. She appeared to him at length and told him that had it not been for his powerful intercession with God, she should have remained an interminable time in Purgatory.

In the Dominican Order it is the rule to pray for the Master Generals by name on their anniversaries. Many of these have been dead several hundred years! They were men especially eminent for piety and learning. This rule would not be approved by the Church were it not necessary and prudent.

We do not mean to imply that all souls are detained equally long periods in the expiatory fires. Many have committed lesser faults and have done more penance. Therefore, their punishment will be much less severe.

Still, the instances we have quoted are very much to the point, for if these souls who enjoyed the intimacy, who saw the example and who shared in the intercession of great Saints during their lives and were aided by their most efficacious suffrages after death were yet detained for such a length of time in Purgatory, what may not happen to us who enjoy none of these wonderful privileges?

Why Such a Lengthy Expiation?

The reasons are not difficult to find: The malice of sin is very great. What appear to us small faults are in reality serious offenses against the infinite goodness of God. It is enough to see how the Saints wept over their faults. We are weak, it may be urged. That is true, but then God offers us abundant graces to strengthen our weakness, gives us light to see the gravity of our faults, and the necessary force to conquer temptation. If we are still weak, the fault is all our own. We do not use the light and strength God so generously offers us; we do not pray, we do not receive the Sacraments as we should.

An eminent theologian wisely remarks that if souls are condemned to Hell for all eternity because of one mortal sin, it is not to be wondered at that other souls should be detained for long years in Purgatory who have committed countless deliberate venial sins, some of which are so grave that at the time of their commission the sinner scarcely knows if they are mortal or venial. Too, they may have committed many mortal sins for which they have had little sorrow and done little or no penance. The guilt has been remitted by absolution, but the pain due to the sins will have to be paid in Purgatory.

Our Lord tells us that we shall have to render an account for each and every idle word we say and that we may not leave our prison until we shall have paid the last farthing. (Cf. Matt. 5:26.)

The Saints committed few and slight sins, and still they sorrowed much and did severe penances. We commit many and grave sins, and we sorrow little and do little or no penance.

Venial Sins

It would be difficult to calculate the immense number of venial sins that any Catholic commits.

There is an infinite number of faults of selflove, selfishness; thoughts, words and acts of sensuality, too, in a hundred forms; faults of charity in thought, word and deed; laziness, vanity, jealousy, tepidity and innumerable other faults.

There are sins of omission which we pay so little heed to. We love God so little, yet He has a thousand claims on our love. We treat Him with coldness, indifference and base ingratitude.

He died for each one of us. Do we ever thank Him as we ought? He remains day and night on the Altar, waiting for our visits, anxious to help us.

How seldom we go to Him! He longs to come into our hearts in Holy Communion, and we refuse Him entrance. He offers Himself up for us on the Altar every morning at Mass and gives oceans of graces to those who assist at the Great Sacrifice. Yet many are too lazy to go to this Calvary! What an abuse of grace!

Our hearts are mean and hard, full of selflove. We have happy homes, splendid food, warm clothing, an abundance of all good things. Many around us live in hunger and misery, and we give them so little; whereas, we spend lavishly and needlessly on ourselves.

Life is given us to serve God, to save our souls. Most Christians, however, are satisfied to give God five minutes of prayer in the morning, five minutes at night! The rest of the 24 hours is given to work, rest and pleasure. Ten minutes to God, to our immortal souls, to the great work we have to do, viz. , our salvation. Twenty-three hours and 50 minutes to this transitory life! Is it fair to God?

It may be alleged that our work, our rest, our sufferings are done for God!

They should be, and then our merits would be indeed great. The truth is that many scarcely ever think of God during the day. The one engrossing object of their thoughts is self. They think and labor and rest and sleep to satisfy self. God gets a very little place in their day and in their minds. This is an outrage to His loving Heart, which is ever thinking of us.

Now Come to Mortal Sins

Many Christians unfortunately commit mortal sins during their lives, but though they confess them, they make no due satisfaction for them, as we have already said.

The Venerable Bede appears to be of the opinion that those who pass a great part of their lives in the commission of grave sins and confess them on their deathbed may be detained in Purgatory even until the Last Day.

St. Gertrude in her revelations states that those who have committed many grave sins and have not done due penance may not share in the ordinary suffrages of the Church for a very considerable time!

All those sins, mortal and venial, are accumulating for the 20, 30, 40, 60 years of our lives. Each and every one has to be atoned for after death.

Is it, then, any wonder that souls have to remain so long in Purgatory?

Why pray for the poor souls?

Our Lord's Great Law is that we must love one another, genuinely and sincerely. The First Great Commandment is to love God with all our heart and soul. The Second, or rather a part of the First, is to love our neighbor as ourselves. This is not a counsel or a mere wish of the Almighty. It is His Great Commandment, the very base and essence of His Law. So true is this that He takes as done to Himself what we do for our neighbor, and as refused to Himself what we refuse to our neighbor.

We read in the Gospel of St. Matthew (Matt. 25:34-46) the words that Christ will address to the just on Judgment Day: Then shall the king say to them that shall be on his right hand: Come, ye blessed of my Father, possess you the kingdom prepared for you from the foundation of the world. For I was hungry, and you gave me to eat; I was thirsty, and you gave me to drink; I was a stranger, and you took me in: Naked, and you covered me: sick, and you visited me: I was in prison, and you came to me. Then shall the just answer him, saying: Lord, when did we see thee hungry, and fed thee; thirsty, and gave thee drink? And when did we see thee a stranger, and took thee in? or naked, and covered thee? Or when did we see thee sick or in prison, and came to thee? And the king answering, shall say to them: Amen I say to you, as long as you did it to one of these my least brethren, you did it to me. Then he shall say to them also that shall be on his left hand: Depart from me, you cursed, into everlasting fire which was prepared for the devil and his angels. For I was hungry, and you gave me not to eat: I was thirsty, and you gave me not to drink. I was a stranger, and you took me not in: naked, and you covered me not: sick and in prison, and you did not visit me. Then they also shall answer him, saying: Lord, when did we see thee hungry, or thirsty, or a stranger, or naked, or sick, or in prison, and did not minister to thee?

Then he shall answer them, saying: Amen I say to you, as long as you did it not to one of these least, neither did you do it to me. And these shall go into everlasting punishment: but the just, into life everlasting.

Some Catholics seem to think that this Law has fallen into abeyance in these days of selfassertion and selfishness, when everyone thinks only of himself and his personal aggrandizement.

"It is useless to urge the Law of Love nowadays," they say, "everyone has to shift for himself, or go under."

No such thing! God's great Law is still and will ever be in full force. Nay, it is more than ever necessary, more than ever our duty and more than ever our own best interest.

We Are Bound to Pray for the Holy Souls

We are always bound to love and help each other, but the greater the need of our neighbor, the more stringent and the more urgent this obligation is. It is not a favor that we may do or leave undone, it is our duty: we must help each other.

It would be a monstrous crime, for instance, to refuse the poor and destitute the food necessary to keep them alive. It would be appalling to refuse aid to one in direst need, to pass by and not extend a hand to save a drowning man. Not only must we help others when it is easy and convenient, but we must make every sacrifice, when need be, to succor our brother in distress.

Now, who can be in more urgent need of our charity than the souls in Purgatory? What hunger or thirst or dire sufferings on this Earth can compare to their dreadful torments? Neither the poor nor the sick nor the suffering we see around us have any such urgent need of our succor. Yet we find many good-hearted people who interest themselves in every other type of suffering, but alas, scarcely one who works for the Holy Souls!

Who can have more claim on us? Among them, too, there may be our mothers and fathers, our friends and near of kin.

God Wishes Us to Help Them

In any event, they are God's dearest friends. He longs to help them; He desires most earnestly to have them in Heaven. They can never again offend Him, and they are destined to be with Him for all Eternity. True, God's justice demands expiation of their sins, but by an amazing dispensation of His Providence He places in our hands the means of assisting them, He gives us the power to relieve and even release them. Nothing pleases Him more than for us to help them. He is as grateful to us as if we had helped Himself.

Our Lady Wants Us to Help Them

Never did a mother of this Earth love so tenderly a dying child, never did she strive so earnestly to soothe its pains, as Mary seeks to console her suffering children in Purgatory, to have them with her in Heaven. We give her unbounded joy each time we take a soul out of Purgatory.

The Holy Souls Will Repay Us a Thousand Times Over

But what shall we say of the feelings of the Holy Souls themselves? It would be utterly impossible to describe their unbounded gratitude to those who help them! Filled with an immense desire to repay the favors done them, they pray for their benefactors with a fervor so great, so intense, so constant that God can refuse them nothing. St. Catherine of Bologna says: "I received many and very great favors from the Saints, but still greater favors from the Holy Souls."

When they are finally released from their pains and enjoy the beatitude of Heaven, far from forgetting their friends on Earth, their gratitude knows no bounds. Prostrate before the Throne of God, they never cease to pray for those who helped them. By their prayers they shield their friends from the dangers and protect them from the evils that threaten them.

They will never cease these prayers until they see their benefactors safely in Heaven, and they will be forever their dearest, sincerest and best friends.

Did Catholics only know what powerful protectors they secure by helping the Holy Souls, they would not be so remiss in praying for them.

The Holy Souls Will Lessen Our Purgatory

Another great grace that they obtain for their helpers is a short and easy Purgatory, or possibly its complete remission!

Saint John Massias, the Dominican lay brother, had a wonderful devotion to the Souls in Purgatory. He obtained by his prayers (chiefly by the recitation of the Rosary) the liberation of one million four hundred thousand souls!

In return, they obtained for him the most abundant and extraordinary graces and came at the hour of his death to help and console him and accompany him to Heaven.

This fact is so certain that it was inserted by the Church in the bull of his beatification.

The learned Cardinal Baronius recounts a similar incident.

He was himself called to assist a dying gentleman. Suddenly, a host of blessed spirits appeared in the chamber of death, consoled the dying man and chased away the devils who sought, by a last desperate effort, to compass his ruin.

When asked who they were, they made answer that they were 8,000 souls whom he had released from Purgatory by his prayers and good works. They were sent by God, so they said, to take him to Heaven without his passing one moment in Purgatory.

St. Gertrude was fiercely tempted by the devil when she came to die. The evil spirit reserves a dangerous and subtle temptation for our last moments. As he could find no other ruse sufficiently clever with which to assail the Saint, he thought to disturb her beautiful peace of soul by suggesting that she would surely remain long years in the awful fires of Purgatory since, he reminded her, she had long ago made over all her suffrages to other souls. But Our Blessed Lord, not content with sending His Angels and the thousands of souls she had released to assist her, came Himself in person to drive away Satan and comfort His dear Saint. He told St. Gertrude that in exchange for all she had done for the Holy Souls, He would take her straight to Heaven and would multiply a hundredfold all her merits.

Blessed Henry Suso, of the Dominican Order, made a compact with a fellow religious to the effect that, when one of the two died, the survivor would offer two Masses each week for his soul, and other prayers as well.

It so fell out that his companion died first, and Blessed Henry commenced immediately to offer the promised Masses. These he continued to say for a long time. At last, quite sure that the soul of his saintly friend had reached Heaven, he ceased offering the Masses.

Great was his sorrow and consternation when the soul of the dead brother appeared to him suffering intensely and chiding him for not celebrating the promised Masses. Blessed Henry replied with deep regret that he had not continued the Masses, believing that his friend must be enjoying the Beatific Vision but he added that he had ever remembered him in prayer.

"O dear Brother Henry, please give me the Masses, for it is the Precious Blood of Jesus that I most need!" cried out the suffering soul. Blessed Henry began anew and, with redoubled fervor, offered Masses and prayers for his friend until he received absolute certitude of his delivery.

Then it was his turn to receive graces and blessings of all kinds from the dear brother he had relieved, and very many times more than he could have expected.

How can we help the Holy Souls?

The first means is by joining the Association of the Holy Souls. The conditions are easy:

a) Have your name registered in the Book of the Association.

b) Hear Mass once a week (Sunday suffices) for the Holy Souls, if possible.

c) Pray for and promote devotion to the Holy Souls.

Those who wish to join and do not have the Association in their parish can send their name, address and annual alms to the Association of the Holy Souls. A second means of helping the Holy Souls is by having Masses offered for them. This is certainly the most efficacious way of relieving them.

Those who cannot get many Masses offered, owing to the want of means, ought to assist at as many Masses as possible for this intention.

A young man who was earning a very modest salary told the writer: "My wife died a few years ago. I got 10 Masses said for her. I could not possibly do more, but heard 1,000 for her dear soul. "

The recital of the Rosary (with its great indulgences) and making the Way of the Cross (which is also richly indulged) are excellent means of helping the Holy Souls.

St. John Massias, as we saw, released from Purgatory more than a million souls, chiefly by reciting the Rosary and offering its great indulgences for them.

Another easy and efficacious way is by the constant repetition of short indulgenced prayers [applying the indulgence to the Souls in Purgatory].

Many people have the custom of saying 500 or 1,000 times each day the little ejaculation, "Sacred Heart of Jesus, I place my trust in Thee!" or the one word, "Jesus. " These are most consoling devotions; they bring oceans of grace to those who practice them and give immense relief to the Holy Souls.

Those who say the ejaculations 1,000 times a day gain 300,000 days Indulgence! What a multitude of souls they can thus relieve! What will it not be at the end of a month, a year, 50 years? And if they do not say the ejaculations, what an immense number of graces and favors they shall have lost! It is quite possible -- and even easy -- to say these ejaculations 1,000 times a day. But if one does not say them 1,000 times, let him say them 500 or 200 times.

Still another powerful prayer is: "Eternal Father, I offer Thee the most Precious Blood of Jesus, with all the Masses being said all over the world this day, for the Souls in Purgatory. "

Our Lord showed St. Gertrude a vast number of souls leaving Purgatory and going to Heaven as a result of this prayer, which the Saint was accustomed to say frequently during the day.

The Heroic Act consists in offering to God in favor of the Souls in Purgatory all the works of satisfaction we practice during life and all the suffrages that will be offered for us after death. If God rewards so abundantly the most trifling alms given to a poor man in His name, what an immense reward will He not give to those who offer all their works of satisfaction in life and death for the Souls He loves so dearly.

This Act does not prevent priests from offering Mass for the intentions they wish, or lay people from praying for any persons or other intentions they desire. We counsel everyone to make this act.

Alms Help the Holy Souls

St. Martin gave half of his cloak to a poor beggar, only to find out afterwards that it was to Christ he had given it. Our Lord appeared to him and thanked him.

Blessed Jordan of the Dominican Order could never refuse to give an alms when it was asked in the Name of God. One day he had forgotten his purse. A poor man implored an alms for the love of God. Rather than refuse him, Jordan, who was then a student, gave him a most precious cincture or "girdle" which he prized dearly. Shortly after, he entered a church and found his cincture encircling the waist of an image of Christ Crucified. He, too, had given his alms to Christ. We all give our alms to Christ.

RESOLUTION
Let us give all the alms we can afford;
Let us have said all the Masses in our power;
Let us hear as many more as is possible;
Let us offer all our pains and sufferings for the relief of the Holy Souls.

We shall thus deliver countless Souls from Purgatory, who will repay us ten thousand times over.

What the Holy Souls do for those who help them

St. Alphonsus Liguori says that, although the Holy Souls cannot merit for themselves, they can obtain for us great graces. They are not, formally speaking, intercessors, as the Saints are, but through the sweet providence of God, they can obtain for us as astounding favors and deliver us from evils, sickness and dangers of every kind.

It is beyond all doubt, as we have already said, that they repay us a thousand times for anything we do for them.

The following facts, a few hundred of which we might quote, are sufficient to show what powerful and generous friends the Holy Souls are.

How A Girl Found Her Mother

A poor servant girl in France named Jeanne Marie once heard a sermon on the Holy Souls which made an indelible impression on her mind. She was deeply moved by the thought of the intense and unceasing sufferings the Poor Souls endure, and she was horrified to see how cruelly they are neglected and forgotten by their friends on Earth.

Among other things the preacher stressed was that many souls who are in reality near to their release -- one Mass might suffice to set them free -- are oftentimes long detained; it may be for years, just because the last needful suffrage has been withheld or forgotten or neglected!

With her simple faith, Jeanne Marie resolved that, cost what it might, she would have a Mass said for the Poor Souls every month, especially for the soul nearest to Heaven. She earned little, and it was sometimes difficult to keep her promise, but she never failed.

On one occasion she went to Paris with her mistress and there fell ill, so that she was obliged to go to the hospital. Unfortunately, the illness proved to be a long one, and her mistress had to return home, hoping that her maid would soon rejoin her. When at last the poor servant was able to leave the hospital, all she had left of her scanty earnings was one franc!

What was she to do? Where to turn? Suddenly, the thought flashed across her mind that she had not had her usual monthly Mass offered for the Holy Souls. But she had only one franc! That was little enough to buy her food.

Yet her confidence that the Holy Souls would not fail her triumphed. She made her way into a church and asked a priest, just about to say Mass, if he would offer it for the Holy Souls. He consented to do so, never dreaming that the modest alms offered was the only money the poor girl possessed. At the conclusion of the

Holy Sacrifice, our heroine left the church. A wave of sadness clouded her face; she felt utterly bewildered.

A young gentleman, touched by her evident distress, asked her if she was in trouble and if he could help her. She told her story briefly, and ended by saying how much she desired work.

Somehow she felt consoled at the kind way in which the young man listened to what she said, and she fully recovered her confidence.

"I am delighted beyond measure," he said, "to help you. I know a lady who is even now looking for a servant. Come with me. " And so saying he led her to a house not far distant and bade her ring the bell, assuring her that she would find work.

In answer to her ring, the lady of the house herself opened the door and inquired what Jeanne Marie required. "Madam, " she said, "I have been told that you are looking for a servant. I have no work and should be glad to get the position. "

The lady was amazed and replied: "Who could have told you that I needed a servant? It was only a few minutes ago that I had to dismiss my maid, and that at a moment's notice. You did not meet her?"

"No, Madam. The person who informed me that you required a servant was a young gentleman. "

"Impossible!" exclaimed the lady. "No young man, in fact no one at all, could have known that I needed a servant. "

"But Madam, "the girl answered excitedly, pointing to a picture on the wall, "that is the young man who told me!"

"Why, child, that is my only son, who has been dead for more than a year!"

"Dead or not, "asserted the girl with deep conviction in her voice, "it was he who told me to come to you, and he even led me to the door. See the scar over his eye; I would know him anywhere. "

Then followed the full story of how, with her last franc, she had had Mass offered for the Holy Souls, especially for the one nearest to Heaven.

Convinced at last of the truth of what Jeanne Marie had told her, the lady received her with open arms. "Come, " she said, "though not as my servant, but as my dear daughter. You have sent my darling boy to Heaven. I have no doubt that it was he who brought you to me."

How a Poor Boy Became a Bishop, A Cardinal and a Saint.

St. Peter Damian lost both father and mother shortly after his birth. One of his brothers adopted him, but treated him with unnatural harshness, forcing him to work hard and giving him poor food and scanty clothing.

One day Peter found a silver piece, which represented to him a small fortune. A friend told him that he could conscientiously use it for him self, as the owner could not be found.

The only difficulty Peter had was to choose what it was he most needed, for he was in sore need of many things.

While turning the matter over in his young mind, it struck him that he could do a still better thing, viz. , have a Mass said for the Holy Souls in Purgatory, especially for the souls of his dear parents. At the cost of a great sacrifice, he put this thought into effect and had the Mass offered.

The Holy Souls repaid his sacrifice most generously. From that day forward a complete change became noticeable in his fortunes.

His eldest brother called at the house where he lived and, horrified at the brutal hardships the little fellow was subjected to, arranged that he be handed over to his own care. He clad him and fed him as his own child, and educated and cared for him most affectionately. Blessing followed upon blessing. Peter's wonderful talents became known, and he was rapidly promoted to the priesthood; sometime after he was raised to the episcopacy and, finally, created Cardinal. Miracles attested his great sanctity, so that after death he was canonized and made a Doctor of the Church.

These wonderful graces came to him after that one Mass said for the Holy Souls.

An Adventure in the Apennines

A group of priests was called to Rome to treat of a grave business matter.

They were bearers of important documents, and a large sum of money was entrusted to them for the Holy Father. Aware that the Apennines, over which they had to pass, were infested by daring bandits, they chose a trusty driver. There was no tunnel through the mountains nor train in those days.

They placed themselves under the protection of the Holy Souls and decided to say a De Profundis every hour for them.

When right in the heart of the mountains, the driver gave the alarm and at the same time lashed the horses into a furious gallop. Looking around, the priests saw fierce bandits at each side of the road with rifles aimed, ready to fire. They were amazed that no shot rang out. They were completely at the mercy of the bandits.

After an hour's headlong flight, the driver stopped and, looking at the priests, said: "I can not understand how we escaped. These desperadoes never spare anyone. "

The Fathers were convinced that they owed their safety to the Holy Souls, a fact that was afterwards confirmed beyond doubt.

When their business was concluded in Rome, one of their number was detained in the Eternal City, where he was appointed chaplain to a prison

Not long after, one of the fiercest brigands in Italy was captured, condemned to death for a long series of murders and was awaiting execution in this prison.

Anxious to gain his confidence, the chaplain told him of several adventures he himself had had and, finally, of his recent escape in the Apennines. The criminal manifested the greatest interest in the story.

When it was ended, he exclaimed: "I was the leader of that band! We thought that you had money and we determined to rob and murder you. An invisible force prevented each and all of us from firing, as we assuredly would have done had we been able. "

The chaplain then told the brigand of how they had placed themselves under the protection of the Holy Souls, and that they ascribed their deliverance to their protection.

The bandit found no difficulty in believing it. In fact, it made his conversion more easy. He died full of repentance.

How Pius IX Cured a Bad Memory

The venerable Pontiff, Pius IX, appointed a holy and prudent religious named Padre Tomaso to be bishop of a diocese. The priest, alarmed at the responsibility put upon him, begged earnestly to be excused.

His protests were in vain. The Holy Father knew his merits.

Overcome with apprehension, the humble religious solicited an audience with the Pope, who received him most graciously. Once more he pleaded earnestly to be excused, but the Pope was immovable.

As a last recourse, Padre Tomaso told the Holy Father that he had a very bad memory, which would naturally prove to be a grave impediment in the high office put upon him.

Pius IX answered with a smile: "Your diocese is very small in comparison with the Universal Church, which I carry on my shoulders. Your cares will be very light in comparison with mine.

"I, too, suffered from a grave defect of memory, but I promised to say a fervent prayer daily for the Holy Souls, who, in return, have obtained for me an excellent memory. Do you likewise, Dear Father, and you will have cause to rejoice. "

The More We Give, the More We Get

A businessman in Boston joined the Association of the Holy Souls and gave a large sum of money annually that prayers and Masses might be said for them.

The Director of the Association was surprised at the gentleman's generosity, for he knew that he was not a rich man. He asked kindly one day if the alms he so generously gave were his own offering or donations which he had gathered from others.

"What I offer, Dear Fathers," the gentleman said, "is my own offering. Be not alarmed. I am not a very rich man, and you may think that I give more than I am able to do. It is not so, for far from losing by my charity, the Holy Souls see to it that I gain considerably more than I give. They are second to none in generosity. "

The Printer of Cologne

The celebrated printer of Cologne, William Freyssen, gives us the following account of how his child and wife were restored to health by the Holy Souls.

William Freyssen got the order to print a little work on Purgatory. When he was correcting the proofs, his attention was caught by the facts narrated in the book. He learned for the first time what wonders the Holy Souls can work for their friends.

Just at that time his son fell grievously ill, and soon the case became desperate. Remembering what he had read about the power of the Holy Souls, Freyssen at once promised to spread, at his own expense, a hundred copies of the book which his firm was printing. To make the promise more solemn, he went to the church and there made his vow. At once a sense of peace and confidence filled his soul. On his return home, the boy, who had been unable to swallow a drop of water, asked for food. Next day he was out of danger and soon completely cured.

At once, Freyssen ordered the books on Purgatory to be distributed, feeling sure that it was the best way to obtain help for the suffering souls, by interesting a hundred people in them. No one who knows what the Poor Souls suffer can refuse to pray for them.

Time passed, and a new sorrow fell to the share of the printer. This time his dear wife was stricken down and, despite every care, grew daily worse. She lost the use of her mind and was almost completely paralyzed, so that the doctor gave up all hope.

The husband, bethinking him of what the Holy Souls had done for his boy, again ran to the church and promised to distribute 200 of the books on Purgatory, begging in exchange the urgent succor of the Holy Souls.

Wonderful to relate, the mental aberration ceased, his wife's mind became normal, and she recovered the use of her limbs and of her tongue. In a short time she was perfectly restored to health.

The Cure of a Cancer

D. Joana de Menezes thus tells of her cure: She was suffering severely from a cancerous growth in the leg and was plunged in grief.

Remembering what she had heard of the power of the Souls in Purgatory, she resolved to place all her confidence in them and had nine Masses offered for them. She promised, moreover, to publish news of her cure if it were granted. Gradually the swelling went down, and the tumor and cancer disappeared.

An Escape From Brigands

Father Louis Manaci, a zealous missionary, had great devotion to the Souls in Purgatory. He found himself obliged to set out on a dangerous journey, but confidently asked the Holy Souls to protect him in the dangers that he was likely to meet with. His road lay through a vast desert, which he knew to be infested with brigands. While plodding along, saying the Rosary for the Holy Souls, what was not his surprise, on looking around, but to find himself surrounded by a bodyguard, as it were, of blessed spirits. Soon he discovered the reason. He had fallen into an ambuscade of brigands, but the Holy Souls at once surrounded him and drove off the miscreants, who sought his life. The Holy Souls did not abandon him until he was well out of danger.

A Return to Life

The Prior of Cirfontaines gives us his story: "A young man of my parish fell dangerously ill with a typhoid fever. His parents were overcome with grief and asked me to recommend him to the prayers of the members of the Association of the Holy Souls.

"It was Saturday. The boy was at death's door. The doctors had had recourse to every remedy. All in vain. They could think of nothing more. They were in despair. "I was the only one who had hope. I knew the power of the Holy Souls, for I had already seen what they could do.

"On Sunday I begged the Associates of the Holy Souls to pray fervently for our sick friend.

"On Monday the danger passed. The boy was cured."

How To Grieve For Your Dead

While it is impossible not to grieve over the loss of one who was greatly cherished, it is possible to learn how to grieve with profit both to yourself and to the one whom death took away from you. There is nothing in human experience that cannot be faced and endured in a right way and a wrong way. The experience of bereavement is no exception to this rule. Only it must be noted that the right way to endure grief over the death of a loved one cannot be learned on the spur of the moment, nor in the sudden hour of its need. It must be mulled over beforehand. The right thoughts that must survive in one's consciousness through the emotional upheaval that goes with bereavement must have been pondered and made familiar long before the need arose.

That is why the thoughts here presented should be considered carefully by all, even those who have never yet seen death fixed on the features of someone very close to them. We can think of only one kind of person who has no need for these thoughts. It is the supremely selfish man and woman who have never forgotten self long enough to love somebody else with a deep and wholehearted love. Such persons do not grieve very much when one close to them is taken by death. There is no need of trying to teach them how to grieve with profit. They need something far more essential; they need to be taught how to forget themselves in true and sincere love of someone else.

Two Very Special Points

Two very special points should be noted here, preliminary to a consideration of the principles that make grief in bereavement profitable. The first is the fact that we are considering only such loves between human beings as are honest and good in the eyes of God. A person who has been living in forbidden and sinful love and companionship with another, and who then suddenly finds the latter taken by death, has reasons for grief far beyond anything that shall be dealt with here. To have contributed to the bad death of a human being, as by living with that person in a sinful alliance or a bad marriage to the very end, is a cause of grief for which there are practically no palliating words that can be said.

The other point is that grief can be turned into profit only where there has been and is genuine faith in God, acceptance of the merits of Christ, convictions of the immortality of the soul, and dedication to the destiny for which God created all human beings. We confess to a sense of utmost futility in speaking to bereaved persons who, together with their deceased loved ones, have had no real faith in God or the reality of another world. At the same time it can be said that a statement of the principles that make the grief of bereavement bearable and profitable [spiritually] for Christians can awaken in pagans a realization of how unnatural and empty are their lives and griefs so long as they turn their eyes away from God and the world that exists beyond the grave. It is hoped that these words will perform that service for many who need.

Motives Mortified Into Joy

The first principle that must be tentaciously clung to in the dark hours and empty days that follow on the death of someone greatly loved, may be phrased as follows:

All human grief arises from a mingling of selfish and unselfish motives. The selfish motives must be mortified; the unselfish motives can be turned into spiritual joy.

Grief arises, first of all, over the loss of something precious. This is a spontaneous thing, and is not to be entirely condemned merely because of the selfish element it contains. No normal human being can help grieving over the loss of a good mother, a loyal father, a faithful husband or wife, a beloved child, a close and dear friend. The loss of something good and dear naturally brings about the reaction of grief in human emotions. Though this cannot be prevented, it helps greatly to be conscious, in the midst of grief, that the selfish motive is present, and to try to temper it as much as possible.

We all like to think, however, that it is not only our loss that causes our grief in breavement. We are so constituted that we do grieve spontaneously out of sympathy for the sufferings of others. That is why people shed tears at a tragic stage show, or if they happen to be present when somebody else is keenly suffering, even though they themselves are but little involved. So, too, when death takes from us someone whom we have greatly loved, our grief will be partly a grief of sympathy. Death, we say, was a misfortune that befell our beloved. Death silenced the voice and froze the hands and stilled the heart of one whom we cherished. We grieve, therefore, not only over what we lost, but also over the terrible thing that happened to the one we lost.

It is here that the realities of faith must take over to temper both the selfish and unselfish elements of our grief. We think of death as a misfortune for two reasons; first, because of what it does to the body, and second, because it is so strong an instinct of our nature to cling to life on earth as a most precious possession. Both these reasons must yield to convictions born of the revealed teachings of the Son of God Himself.

Death does treat the body cruelly, but it brings about a great release, a happy liberation, for the soul. The very coldness and stillness of a body in death should be a reminder of the new freedom and exaltation of the soul. If the eyes could see and the hands still move and the heart still beat, the soul would still be there. That the body can no longer act must be a reminder even to those whose eyes are blinded by tears that the soul is elsewhere, and that it now has a knowledge and love to which all that it had while united to the body cannot even dimly be compared.

It is true, too, that all human instincts resist death and cling to life, so that one who dies may be said to have failed in his battle to hold body and soul together. But even though one whom we loved did try to cling to life to the instant when death occurred, it must never be forgotten that immediately after death every good Christian finds himself infinitely better off than he was in this world. He knows then that his battles are over; his loves are purified and exalted; his sufferings, if any remain to be endured in purgatory, are but a pledge of most certain and unlimited happiness. With far deeper meaning than is sometimes put into the words of those bereaved, it can be said of those who have died in the Lord that "they would not want to come back again." This must be said even of a child whose soul death has taken from this world.

Thus pity and sympathy for the good dead turn out, in the light of faith, to be unrealistic and misplaced. What is left is the sense of the loss to ourselves. We cannot smother this nor even hide it. It irresistibly charges our feelings and emotions with pain. But in the depths of the soul, where convictions born of faith remain strong, there is comfort and hope and peace.

Deeds of Mercy for the Dead

There is a second principle which, when remembered and made conscious in the midst of the grief of bereavement, helps to bring solace and peace. It may be worded as follows:

Human grief in bereavement is intensified by the remembrance of hurts that were inflicted on the one who cannot suffer such hurts any more. This feature of one's grief should be turned into deeds of mercy for the dead that will far outweigh the hurts that were given in life.

All human loves on earth are imperfect.

Two people who love each other dearly, even husband and wife, mother and son, brother and sister, friend and friend, inevitably find over the course of the years that they sometimes hurt each other. It may be by thoughtlessness or neglect; or through misunderstanding or difference of opinion; or as a result of sensitiveness or impatience. The hurts inflicted may range from the momentary ones resulting from a sudden harsh word or gesture, to the long enduring heartaches that survive bitter quarrels or downright sins. Love is rarely experienced for very long on earth without some heartache and pain.

This is a proof to the thoughtful that human beings were made for the perfect loves of heaven, and that they shall never know an all-satisfying love until they have won that goal. It is also a reminder to those who have been bereaved that they are now to make up for the slights and hurts that they inflicted on the one who has now been taken from them. They cannot slight or hurt, as they did before, their beloved dead any more. But the memory of the past shortcomings of their own love can be turned into wonderful deeds of charity and mercy in behalf of their dead.

Indeed, this seems to be one of the reasons why God does not reveal to the living when or how soon the souls of their dead will be admitted into heaven. He wants true love and deeds of mercy to continue for a long time after death — even till a reunion is enjoyed in heaven. He wants love's wounds to be healed in death. He wants the memory of the imperfections of one's love to send forth into eternity a continuing flow of prayers and meritorious offerings that will speed the beloved's passage through purgatory and add to his happiness in heaven as the imperfections of earthly love continue to be atoned.

Without this principle there is too often an element of hypocrisy in a show of grief at the death of one who was close and dear. A son who often hurt his mother deeply during her life may act at her death as if his was always a perfect and unselfish love. A daughter who was given to quarreling often with her mother while the latter was alive may manifest uncontrollable grief at her mother's death. A great variety of motives and feelings enter into such displays. We tend to idealize the dead and to grieve for the ideal we lost. Consciousness of our own faults toward the dead make remorse a part of our grief. Even human respect, in the form of a desire to grieve as the world expects of those who have lost a loved one, plays its part. But all the mixed emotions that come together in grief over the corpse of one who was close and dear, bear wonderful fruit if they are directed toward the deeds of mercy for the dead that both atone for the faults of the still living and pay the penalty still due for the faults of the dead.

Valuable Reminders

The third principle that takes some of the sharp sting out of bereavement may take the following form:

Death is always a valuable reminder to the living, and especially to those who have loved the one whom death has taken, of the shortness and uncertainty of life on earth, of the importance of living in such a manner that death need not be feared, and of the joyous reunion that will take place between those who have been separated by death for a little while.

Nothing is permitted by God to happen to one human being that is not intended as a lesson to others. This is so because of the identity of the destiny that all men are created to achieve, and of many of the means to its attainment. All men are made to win heaven through the manner of their living on earth; the end of one person's living on earth should remind others who witness it, of their own principal goal. All men must die, even though many like to live in forgetfulness of the fact; the death of one breaks through that forgetfulness and drives home the salutary truth that death cannot be evaded. All men are to win heaven only by loyalty to God and true faith in Christ on earth; the death of one who was loyal and faithful is a reminder to the living of the only source of hope on which they can rely.

The closer one has been to a person who dies, the greater should be the force of these lessons. All death are lessons to the living, but the death of loved ones are like direct and inescapable reminders from God of the most important things. That is because the death of a loved one punctures the dangerous dream to which all are tempted to succumb, that life on earth may be sweet enough to cling to without thought of heaven. The longer God permits true love to be enjoyed on earth, the more He risks permitting His children to be deceived. Inevitably He lets death speak for Him sooner or later, to tell them that they must not turn astray from their true goal.

This is one of God's purposes in permitting death to strike into the midst of happy families, or to sever friend from friend. It is evident in the fact that death often brings about wonderful conversions in the living that nothing else seemed capable of effecting. The wayward children of good mothers are sometimes brought to their senses and inspired to give up their sins only when they see that mother's features fixed and peaceful in death.

Men and women who had thought they needed nothing but the little circle of human friends, found themselves suddenly realizing their need of God when He has reached down and taken one most beloved out of that circle.

This requires humility, of course. Proud men and women become only embittered when they have to face the death of a dear one. Humble people recognize God's supreme rights and His infinite wisdom in death, even though they had been thinking little about them before. And they permit their thoughts to go out of this world with the one whom God took to Himself, until those thoughts rest with the loved one in God.

Added to the force of this lesson are the thoughts that inescapably come to those who are left to grieve over the death of one whom they loved. The first consists in the right answer to the question, "Do the dead still know and think about and love us to whom they were bound by love on earth?" The right answer to this question is yes, they do. God does not inspire the close relationships that true and virtuous love creates between human beings on earth only to smash and destroy them at death. Love is God's creation; He gave it the instinct and longing for permanence; it can be taken for granted that even in the bleak and silent separation that death effects, He permits the dead to think of the living as the living cannot help thinking of the dead. Who will not be a better man or woman if the solid conviction is possessed that those whom they have loved and lost are not really lost, but are thinking of them in the presence of God in another world?

The second thought that makes the lessons of death more profitable is that which arises from the right answer to the question, "Shall I ever see this loved one again?" The answer again is yes, provided you live in such a way as to deserve a union with God and a reunion with your lost loved ones when your life is over. Death plays a wonderful part in God's plans for the salvation of all men when it inspires the bereaved living to say with all possible resoluteness of soul: "I shall now make straight for heaven where my loved one waits; I shall never be turned aside from that goal any more." The waiting period will seem short and swiftly passing for one who has thus fixed his eyes on its glorious end.

Harmful Attitudes

There are two harmful attitudes toward the death of a beloved person that must be considered in conjunction with the right principles set down above.

The first is the attitude of self-recrimination that some bereaved persons fall into, on the score that they did not do enough, or failed to do some simple things, that might have prevented the death over which they grieve.

Too often people torture themselves with thoughts like these concerning their dead: "If only I had recognized the symptoms of his disease when they first appeared, he would be alive today." Or, "If only I had called a doctor a month earlier, his life would have been saved." Or, "It was my fault that he died because I did not insist that he give up working."

This self-accusation takes its most acute form when death was due to an accident, whether the grieving person played an unconscious part in the accident or not. Over and over, in agonizing detail, such a person will think of how small a thing, what little watchfulness and care, would have prevented the tragedy that occurred.

This wrong attitude, to which all bereaved persons are tempted to succumb, except sometime in the case of the death of the very old, can be exorcised only by reflexion on and faith in the providence of God. As responsible human beings, we are bound to do, indeed we can do, only the things that our conscience tells us are practically prudent and morally necessary here and now. If we neglected something, without any consciousness of neglect, that seems, after the event, to have had some bearing on a loved one's death, we are bound to see the wise and loving hand of God's providence in the event that occurred. Even when there was some conscious neglect but without realization of how serious the consequences might be, it must, after the fact, be accepted as part of God's plan that the death of one we loved should take place at this time and in this particular way. If, as Our Lord said, He has numbered the hairs of our head, He has also watched over the circumstances that led to anyone's death.

The second wrong attitude that sometimes leads not only to prolonged grieving but also to a habit of sin is that which arises from the thought that it was the neglect or mistake of someone else that occasioned the death of a loved one. The doctor did not come at once when he was called; or he made a wrong diagnosis; or he prescribed a medicine that, instead of helping the patient, seemed to hasten death. Bereaved persons sometimes permit their grief to turn into a hatred of such a physician. We know of cases in which such persons have refused for years to speak to the doctor who was called for their mother or father or husband or wife because the patient died, and who have done all they could to harm the professional reputation of that doctor.

No one would say that the neglect or mistaken diagnosis of a physician never enters into the chain of circumstances that lead to death. But only one who is very proud in his own judgment, and forgetful of Christian principles, would set it down as certain that in a particular case this was actually the sole cause of death. And even where there are some grounds for believing that someone's neglect or carelessness may have contributed to the death of a loved one, it must be remembered that even such things could not happen except they were wisely permitted by the providence of God. There are no accidents with God; He permits nothing to happen that is not taken into His universal plan.

For this reason it is tragic for bereaved persons to permit the death of one whom they love to lead to hatred and detraction. If someone else sinned by neglect, it does no good to an individual who suffers from the result of that neglect to pile other sins on top of that sin. This only makes grief bitter and unprofitable and vain, when it might have borne great fruit both for the one who died and the one who was bereaved.

How To Avoid Purgatory

We are created for eternal happiness in heaven, so we are obliged to set our course straight to heaven. Jesus tells us "be ye perfect." (Matthew 5:48) Our goal is perfection and with God's help, we can achieve perfection. The Saints did it and we are all called to be Saints. So let us get about becoming Saints and avoiding not only Hell, but also Purgatory. Let us consider that Purgatory is not for sinners, but for those who don't quite make it to sainthood on earth, but are striving for perfection. If we look at it this way we will tackle our pet sins and eliminate them from our lives. If not, then we will risk hell by being lax in our fight against the world, the flesh and the devil. Recall we are the Church Militant, as the Catechism teaches us. We are in a warfare for our soul. If we win the war, we obtain heaven, if we lose, we condemn ourself to hell for all eternity. Consider this well, my friend, where do you want to be a trillion years from now?

Let us remind ourselves of the duty to meditate daily on the truths of our Holy Faith. Remember the Saints tell us that we will either give up sin or we will give up meditation. We can consider meditation as heaven insurance.

Resignation to the Death God Wills for Us

Trustful Surrender to Divine Providence

Even more, it is the teaching of great masters of the spiritual life that a person who, at the point of death, makes an act of perfect conformity to the will of God will be delivered not only from hell but also from purgatory, even if he has committed all the sins in the world. "The reason," says St. Alphonsus, "is that he who accepts death with perfect resignation acquires similar merit to that of a martyr who has voluntarily given his life for Christ, and even amid the greatest sufferings he will die happily and joyfully."

From Saint Alphonsus

"Happy you if you do the same that is, if you are always resigned to the divine will. Truly happy shall be your life, and still more happy your death. Blosius says that he who, at the moment of death, makes an act of perfect conformity to the divine will, shall be delivered not only from hell, but also from purgatory, though he had been guilty of all the sins of the whole world. The reason is, that he who accepts death with perfect resignation acquires merit similar to that of the holy martyrs who spontaneously gave their lives for Jesus Christ. Moreover, he who dies with perfect conformity to the divine will dies in peace and joy, even in the midst of pains. A Cistercian monk was seized with his last illness; his flesh became rotten, and his pains were so excruciating that he suffered a continual death; but the good religious unceasingly thanked the Lord, and enjoyed uninterrupted tranquility and consolation. When near his last breath, and racked with increased torture, he began to sing. The monks that stood round his bed were astonished to see such joy amid so many pains; but his cheerfulness continued to the last moment, and thus, with joy and jubilation, he happily closed his life.

When you, dear sister, are visited by God with any infirmity, or loss, or persecution, humble yourself, and say with the good thief, We receive the due reward of our deeds. Lord, I deserve this cross because I have offended Thee. Humble yourself and be comforted: for the chastisement that you receive is a proof that God wishes to pardon the eternal punishment due to your sins. Who will grant me, says Job, . . . that this may be my comfort, that afflicting me with sorrow, He spare not." Let this be my consolation, that the Lord may afflict me and may not spare me here below in order to spare me hereafter. O God! how can he who has deserved hell complain if the Lord send him a cross. Were the pains of hell trifling, still, because they are eternal, we should gladly exchange them for all temporal sufferings that have an end. But no: in hell there are all kinds of pain they are all intense and everlasting. And though you should have preserved baptismal innocence and have never deserved hell, you have at least merited a long purgatory: and do you know what purgatory is? St. Thomas says that the souls in purgatory are tormented by the very fire that tortures the damned. Hence St. Augustine says that the pain of that fire surpasses every torment that man can suffer in this life. Be content, then, to be chastised in this life rather than in the next; particularly since by accepting crosses with patience in this life your sufferings will be meritorious; but hereafter you will suffer without merit.

Recapitulation

Saint Pius X indulgenced the following prayer of resignation to the death God wills of us: "Eternal Father, from this day forward, I accept with a joyful and resigned heart the death it will please You to send me, with all its pains and sufferings." Let us resign ourself wholly to God's most holy will in death and in all things, as we pray in the Our Father, "Thy will be done."

The Desire For Heaven

Saint Alphonsus says: "It is said that in purgatory those souls who in this life have had but little longing for heaven are punished with a particular suffering, called the pain of languor; and with reason, because to long but little for heaven is to set small value on the great good of the eternal kingdom which our Redeemer has purchased for us by his death. Forget not, therefore, devout soul, frequently to sigh after heaven: say to your God that it seems to you an endless time for you to come and see him, and to love him face to face. Long ardently to depart out of this banishment, this scene of sinning, and danger of losing his grace, that you may arrive in that land of love where you may love him with all your powers. Say to him again and again, Lord, so long as I live on this earth, I am always in danger of forsaking Thee and losing Thy love. When will it be that I quit this life, wherein I am ever offending Thee, and come to love Thee with all my soul, and unite myself to Thee, with no danger of losing Thee any more? St. Teresa was ever sighing in this way, and used to rejoice when she heard the clock strike, because another hour of life, and of the danger of losing God, was past and gone. For she so greatly desired death in order to see God, that she was dying with the desire to die; and hence she composed that loving canticle of hers, I die, because I do not die."

Many have a lax attitude in regard to life. Live with one foot in the world and one foot in the Church. We wish to be just enough in the Church to avoid hell, while remaining attached to the world and enjoying as many pleasures as we can. This is a dangerous attitude.

Purge All Attachments to the World

Saint Catherine of Genoa says: "And thus this blessed Soul, illuminated by the divine ray, said: "Would that I could utter so strong a cry that it would strike all men with terror, and say to them: O wretched beings! why are you so blinded by this world that you make, as you will find at the hour of death, no provision for the great necessity that will then come upon you?

"You shelter yourselves beneath your hope in the mercy of God, which you unceasingly exalt, not seeing that it is your resistance to His great goodness which will be your condemnation. His goodness should constrain you to His will, not encourage you to persevere in your own. Since His justice is unfailing it must needs be in some way fully satisfied.

"Have not the boldness to say: 'I will go to confession and gain a plenary indulgence and thus I shall be saved.' Remember that the full confession and entire contrition which are requisite to gain a plenary indulgence are not easily attained. Did you know how hardly they are come by, you would tremble with fear and be more sure of losing than of gaining them."

And Fr. Schouppe says in <u>Purgatory</u>: "Happily before death I confessed my sins in such dispositions as to escape Hell, but now I suffer here to expiate the worldly life that my mother did not prevent me from leading! Alas! This head, which loved to be adorned, and which sought to draw the attention of others, is now devoured with flames within and without, and these flames are so violent that every moment it seems to be that I must die. These shoulders, these arms, which I loved to see admired, are cruelly bound in chains of red-hot iron. These feet, formerly trained for the dance, are now surrounded with vipers that tear them with their fangs and soil them with their filthy slime, all these members which I have adorned with jewels, flowers, and divers other ornaments, are now a prey to the most horrible torture. O mother, mother! How culpable you have been in my regard! It was you who, by a fatal indulgence, encouraged my taste for display and extravagant expense; it was you that took me to theaters, parties, and balls, and to those worldly assemblies which are the ruin of souls. If I have not incurred eternal damnation, it was because a special grace of God's mercy touched my heart with sincere repentance. I made a good confession, and thus I have been delivered from Hell, yet only to see myself precipitated into the most horrible torments of Purgatory!"

In the Rosary we pray on the Third Joyful Mystery: "Let us pray for detachment from earthly things." In the Sorrowful Mysteries we pray for three important things. "The Agony in the Garden – let us pray for true contrition for our sins. The Scourging at the Pillar – let us pray for mortification of our bodily senses. The Crowning With Thorns – let us pray for contempt of the world." A spiritual author reminds us that mortification is the enemy of pleasure and pleasure seeking condemns many souls to Hell and many more to Purgatory. Saint Paul reminds us: "she that lives in pleasures is dead while she is alive." (I Timothy 5:6) Another author tells us: "Mortification is the curbing of self-love in all its internal and external manifestations. It is necessary for the **purgation** of the soul, this being a necessary preparation for perfect union with God." Notice the word *purgation*, hence mortification is basically a *little purgatory*, which if we are willing to do here on earth will shorten or even eliminate the need of going to Purgatory after death.

Saint Alphonsus says: "The unhappy soul will then say: Had I mortified myself by not looking at such an object; ... if I had read a spiritual book every day;" How many of us spend hours a day staring at a pretty little box, while it mesmerizes us and spews forth *entertainment*. Of this Saint Alphonsus says: "he who is wholly absorbed with the attractions of the theater" (and the television is a *home theater*) "and ballroom can have no valid claim to the title of faithful Catholic." How many of us will spend centuries expiating this wasted time; time, which could have been spent in something useful, such as prayer and penance? And this does not consider the fact that much of what is on television is sinful to watch, not to mention the fact that the amount of television the average American watches is sinful in and of itself. And this is only one common attachment people have today. It is time to unplug from the world! Meditate well on this. Make a list of your attachments to the world and start pulling the plugs.

Detest All of Our Sins, Mortal and Venial

Saint Joseph Cafasso says: "You may regard a person as already fallen, who wishes to satisfy himself excessively in everything, and to abstain only from what is certainly sinful." Let us consider what Purgatory is for. We know hell is for anyone who has one or more unrepented mortal sins on their soul. Heaven is for the perfect. Purgatory, therefore is those who do not merit hell, but also do not merit heaven immediately at death.

First of all there is the temporal punishment due to our forgiven sins that must repaid. We repay this by prayer, penance and indulgences here on earth or by suffering in Purgatory. And how much penance is sufficient to atone for all of our sins? Recall we have repented of them, but there is still penance to be done for them.

Then there are our unrepented venial sins, that is venial sins we have not repented of, for no sin is forgiven that is not hated. And there are two types of venial sin. The first type are venial sins of weakness as Sacred Scripture says: "For a just man shall fall seven times and shall rise again: but the wicked shall fall down into evil." (Proverbs 24:16) These we cannot totally eliminate, but will fall into although we detest them. We may fall into one at the moment of death and thus have to spend a short time in Purgatory.

After mortal sin, the most dangerous sin is deliberate venial sin. These are sins that we willfully commit, and thus only differ from mortal sin in one aspect, the seriousness of the matter. Because we usually acquire a habit of such sins, we weaken the soul and make it more prone to fall eventually into mortal sin! These sins are also dangerous, because instead of hating them, we love them. Since we love them, we can never be forgiven them, because no sin is forgiven that is not hated. How many will regret their habits of sin, which they considered mere trifles here on earth while in fact they are spending centuries expiating them in Purgatory? Something to meditate on!

How to Gain a Plenary Indulgence

We read in many pious books about gaining indulgences. For instance, making the Stations of the Cross, while meditating on the fourteen Stations has a plenary indulgence attached. Many other pious practices have plenary indulgences attached. However, what is required beyond the performance of the pious exercises?

Saint Joseph Cafasso says: "The condition for gaining a plenary indulgence presents the difficulty that to gain it in full a person must be free from all affection to venial sin." And the <u>Baltimore Catechism</u> reminds us: "Gaining a plenary indulgence requires proper dispositions, as you may understand from its very great advantages. To gain it we must not only hate sin and be heartily sorry even for our venial sins, but we must not have a desire for even venial sin. We should always try to gain a plenary indulgence, for in so doing we always gain at least part of it, or a partial indulgence, greater or less according to our dispositions." This is why we must hate all sin and purge it all from our lives.

How to Avoid Purgatory

Can We Avoid Purgatory? Yes.

Many think that it is practically impossible for the ordinary Christian to avoid Purgatory. Go there we all must--so they say.

They laughingly remark: "It will be well for us if we ever get there"

Alas! When too late they will recognize how terribly rash their words were. As a consequence of such fatalistic ideas, many make no serious effort to avoid Purgatory, or even to lessen the term they may have to pass there. Thank God all do not hold such gloomy views.

WE SHALL STRIVE IN THE FOLLOWING PAGES TO SHOW a) How all can notably shorten their period of expiation in Purgatory; b) And how they may even avoid Purgatory altogether. These pages are well worth reading and re-reading. The fact is that a great number of souls go to Purgatory and remain there for long years simply because they had never been told how they could have avoided it.

The means we suggest are easy, practical and within the reach of all.

Moreover, far from being irksome, the use of these means will only serve to make our lives on this earth holier and happier and will take away the exaggerated fear of death which terrifies so many.

We ask you, Dear Reader, to put this little booklet into the hands of all your friends. You cannot do them a greater service.

How Can We Avoid Purgatory?

The reason why we have to pass through Purgatory after death is that we have committed sins and have not made satisfaction for them. Every individual sin must be expiated--in this life or the next! Not even the slightest shadow of sin or evil can enter the all-holy presence of God.

The graver, the more frequent the sins, the longer will be the period of expiation and the more intense the pain.

It is not God's fault, nor God's wish, that we go to Purgatory! The fault is all our own.

We have sinned and have not made satisfaction.

Even after our sin, God, in His infinite goodness, places at our disposal many easy and efficacious means by which we may considerably lessen our term of expiation, or even entirely cancel it.

Most Christians, with incomprehensible rashness, neglect these means and so have to pay their debts in the dreadful prison house of Purgatory.

We will briefly enumerate some of the principal means by which we can avoid Purgatory-or at least lessen its severity and duration.

The First Means: Removing the Cause

The First Means of avoiding Purgatory is manifestly to remove the cause which sends us there, which is sin.

It may not be easy to refrain from all sin, even the smaller sins, but every ordinary Christian can, by the frequent use of the Sacraments, easily abstain from mortal sin.

Secondly, we can all avoid deliberate and grave venial sin. It is an awful thing to offend the good God deliberately. Deliberation intensifies enormously the malice of sin and offends God much more than faults of weakness, or sins committed when we are off our guard.

Lastly, we must use our best endeavours to break off bad habits. Habits, like deliberation, add seriously to the malice of sin.

A deliberate falsehood is very much worse than a hasty lie of excuse, and a lie resulting from the inveterate habit of lying is very much worse than a casual lie.

A lady once told us how she had, when younger, the habit of constantly speaking ill of her neighbours.

Having heard a sermon on the subject, she made a strong resolution never to do so again, and kept it.

That simple, strong resolution changed the whole trend of her life and saved her from thousands of sins, and most surely from a long and painful Purgatory.

Who cannot make a like resolution and keep it?

If a Christian avoids, as he easily can, these three classes of sin, viz. , mortal sins, deliberate and grave venial sins, and habits of sin, it will be relatively easy for him to atone for faults of frailty, as we shall presently see.

Resolution: We would be well advised to pronounce with special emphasis and fervour, every time we say the Our Father, the words: "Forgive us our trespasses as we forgive those who trespass against us"

These are the very words of God Himself and repeated frequently and fervently will certainly obtain for us pardon of our sins.

The Second Means: Penance

The Second Means of avoiding Purgatory is to satisfy for our sins in this life by doing penance. "Do penance or you shall all likewise perish" Do penance, or you will burn long years in Purgatory, is a fact that there is no getting away from.

This is a terrifying thought and one that makes the bravest man shudder. Which of us does not tremble when he thinks of those who have been burnt to death in a slow fire? What fear would not be ours if we had to face a similar death? Yet their suffering was of relatively short duration. The incomparably fiercer fire of Purgatory, which we may have to face, may last 20, or 50 or 100 years!

Many people have such a horror of penance that they never even dream of practicing it. It is like the fear that children have of ghosts, a very great but a very unfounded fear. Their idea is that penance is something awful. They think perhaps of the severe penances of the great Saints and of course are afraid to attempt anything of a like kind.

God does not ask us, as a rule, to do what is heroic. When He does, He gives us all the strength necessary, as in the case of the Saints. He asks each one to do a little. If we are afraid of doing much, and it is only natural that some should be, let us do at least a little. No one but a coward is afraid to do a little, especially if he gets much in exchange.

The easy road to Heaven of Saint Therese, the Little Flower, is to do many little things. God was infinitely pleased with the widow's mite; He will be equally pleased with our little penances.

As a result of little mortifications, we can deliver ourselves from the awful fires of Purgatory and amass rich merits for Heaven. To go into the matter further, there is not much difficulty about mortification or penance, notwithstanding the absurd fear that people have of it.

Penance is not only easy, it is useful and necessary, and it will bring us very great happiness. Not to do penance is the greatest penance of all. As a matter of fact, every man of the world naturally, spontaneously mortifies himself. The first principle, for instance, of politeness and good breeding is to sacrifice our whims and tastes for the sake of others. The selfish man is a boor; the generous man is the idol of all.

Again, the only way of securing good health is to eschew the most appetizing viands when they do us harm and to make use of plain foods when they do us good. Overeating is the cause of the vast majority of sickness and premature deaths.

To take another example. The secret of success is strenuous, methodical, regular work. Now generosity, self-denial, method, regularity are other forms of very genuine but practical mortification. Yet no man can get on without them. To insist on our own likes and dislikes, to do only as we please, is to lead a life bristling with difficulties, in which every duty is a burden, every good act an effort and a labor.

Boy scouts and girl scouts are bound to do a kind act every day, even though it costs them a big effort. Christians should surely do more. Daily acts of self-restraint, of patience with others, of kindness to others, the exact fulfillment of duty are splendid penances and a great aid to happiness.

Resolution: If we are afraid to do much, let us do many little things.

The Third Means: Suffering

The Third Means of avoiding Purgatory is very easy. It consists in making a virtue of necessity, by bearing patiently what we cannot avoid, and all the more since suffering, borne patiently, becomes easy and light. Suffering, if accepted with calmness and for God's sake, loses all its sting. If received badly, in the spirit of revolt and with repugnance, it is intensified a hundredfold, and becomes almost intolerable.

Everyone in this vale of tears has to face sorrows innumerable and infinite in variety. Crosses light and crosses heavy are the lot of us all. Strange as it may seem, these sorrows, which most of us would gladly dispense with, are in truth God's greatest graces. They are the little share He offers us of His Passion and which He asks us to bear for love of Him and as penance for our sins.

Borne in this spirit they will lessen considerably our time in Purgatory and very possibly completely remove it--with this difference, that Purgatory, even a Purgatory of 50 or 100 years, will in no wise increase our merits in Heaven; whereas, every pain and sorrow and disappointment in this life will lessen our suffering in Purgatory, and also bring us more happiness and glory in Heaven.

How sad it is that so many Christians, for want of thought, make their sufferings a thousand times worse than they are and lose all the immense merits that they could so easily gain.

Resolution: Let us suffer with calmness and serenity for the love of God. We shall thus save ourselves from Purgatory.

The Fourth Means: Confession, Communion, Holy Mass

The Fourth Means by which we can lessen our time in Purgatory, or avoid it altogether, is by frequent Confession, Communion and daily assistance at Mass.

Confession applies to our souls the Precious Blood of Christ, wipes out our sins, gives us light to see their malice, fills us with horror of sin and, above all, it gives us strength to avoid it. In Holy Communion we receive the God of infinite mercy and love, the God of all sanctity, who comes expressly to pardon our sins and help us to sin no more.

Jesus visited the house of Zaccheus once, and in that one visit, Zaccheus obtained complete pardon of all his sins.

How is it possible that the same God of goodness and sweetness can come, not into our houses, but into our very hearts in Holy Communion and not give us the same and even greater graces. He visited Zaccheus once, He visits us every day if we allow Him.

Many, alas, never feel, never grasp the immense joys and consolation of Holy Communion.

The Mass is identical with the Sacrifice of Calvary, in its essence, in its value, in the graces it bestows. The Sacrifice of Calvary was sufficient to save all the world, millions and millions of souls, and was also sufficient to save countless other sinful worlds, had they existed.

By assisting at Mass, we can apply all these oceans of graces to our own souls, and that not once, but every day.

Resolution: Let us go to Mass and Holy Communion every day. We can do nothing better. One day with Mass and Communion is worth a hundred days without them.

The Fifth Means: Asking God

The Fifth Means of avoiding Purgatory is asking God for this grace. Some wise Catholics have a really great, if simple secret, which is well worth learning and using for our own benefit.

God promises us in the most solemn and deliberate way (and He cannot fail to do what He promises) that He will give us everything we ask in prayer, if it is good for us.

Now two conditions, especially, make prayer infallible, namely perseverance and faith. God cannot refuse such a prayer.

These Catholics we speak of pray expressly every day of their lives that God will free them from Purgatory. In every single prayer they say, in every Mass they hear, in every good act they perform, they have the express intention of asking God first of all and with all their hearts to deliver them from Purgatory.

How? That is for God to decide.

It is not easy to see how God can possibly refuse such constant, unceasing prayer. The fact that such prayers are said daily and many times in the day, for 20, 30, 50 years, shows that they are said with undoubting faith and magnificent perseverance.

We exhort all our readers to adopt this practice. The more they know and think on Purgatory, the more fervently will they make this prayer.

Resolution: Every time we say the Hail Mary let us say with all the fervour of our hearts the words: "Pray for us sinners now and at the hour of our death. Amen"

A Sixth Means: Resignation to Death

A Sixth Means of avoiding Purgatory is given us by some great saints: They say that when a sick person becomes aware that he is dying and offers to God his death with perfect resignation, it is very likely that he will go straight to Heaven.

Death is the awful punishment of sin, and when we accept it, as of course we ought to do, with submission and resignation, our act pleases God so much that it may satisfy perfectly for all our sins.

The idea of Pope St. Pius X was the same when he granted a plenary indulgence at the hour of death to those who say at least after one Holy Communion the following prayer: "Eternal Father, from this day forward, I accept with a joyful and resigned heart the death it will please You to send me, with all its pains and sufferings.

It will be better still to say this prayer after every Holy Communion we receive.

It is for our best interest to accept God's will in everything that happens to us in life and in death.

Nothing can be easier when we remember that God always wishes what is best for us. If we do what God does not will, we shall surely suffer.

Resolution: Each time we repeat the Our Father, let us say with special fervour the words: Thy will be done. In all our troubles, small and great, let us do likewise. Thus everything will gain us merit. By this simple act we change sorrow into joy, the worries of life into gold for Heaven.

Act of Resignation to the Divine Will: O Lord my God, I now at this moment readily and willingly accept at Thy hand whatever kind of death it may please Thee to send me, with all its pains, penalties and sorrows.

The Seventh Means: Extreme Unction

The Seventh Means of avoiding Purgatory is Extreme Unction: God Himself has given us a Sacrament, the end of which is to take us directly to Heaven. This Sacrament is Extreme Unction, which according to St. Thomas and St. Albert was instituted especially to obtain for us the grace of a holy and happy death and to prepare us for immediate entrance into Heaven.

Many Catholics do not understand this most consoling doctrine, and because they do not understand it, they prepare themselves insufficiently for the reception of Extreme Unction and so lose many of its great graces.

Every Sacrament properly received produces its effect. Baptism cleanses us from Original Sin and any other actual sins that may have been committed by adults before receiving the Sacrament.

The Sacrament of Holy Orders gives a priest all his tremendous powers. Matrimony makes man and woman husband and wife. In the same way Extreme Unction, if devoutly received, prepares the dying Christian for immediate entrance into Heaven, thus delivering him from Purgatory.

How foolish it is, therefore, to put off receiving this Sacrament until very late, when the dying person is too exhausted to receive it with full knowledge of what he is doing and with due fervour and devotion. The moment of death is the supreme moment in our lives. It is the moment which decides our fate for all Eternity.

Resolution: Let us use every means in our power to secure a happy and holy death, especially by receiving most devoutly, and as soon as possible, Extreme Unction.

Indulgences and Purgatory

God in His infinite mercy and compassion offers us a most wonderful and easy means for lessening or canceling our Purgatory.

Fully aware of our weakness, and knowing, too, how fearful many are of penance, He opens wide the treasury of His Goodness and offers us most abundant Indulgences in exchange for some small act of devotion.

For one recitation of short ejaculatory prayers, He grants 100 or 300 or more days Indulgence. These we may say hundreds of times in the day. Those who say the little ejaculation: "Sacred Heart of Jesus, I place my trust in Thee" one hundred times a day gain 30,000 days Indulgence. Those who say it 1,000 times, as many do, gain 300,000 days Indulgence each day!

Nothing can be easier than to acquire the habit of saying this little prayer all day long, countless times each day.

Then, for each Hail Mary of the Rosary, one gains more than 2,000 days Indulgence!

Besides an immense number of Partial Indulgences, there are very many Plenary (full, complete) Indulgences which may be gained during life and at the hour of death.

These are specially given by the Church to enable us to avoid Purgatory.

These Indulgences can be applied to our own souls, and we shall thus directly make satisfaction for our sins. Or, we may apply them to the souls in Purgatory, who will see to it that we do not lose by our generosity.

Resolution: Let us strive to gain all possible Indulgences.

The Third Orders

Among the extraordinary graces which Catholics gain by becoming members of a Third Order is a share in many Masses and prayers.

To mention, for instance, the Third Order of Saint Dominic, Pope Benedict XV, himself a Tertiary, said: "One of the easiest and most effectual ways of reaching a high degree of sanctity is by becoming a Dominican Tertiary"

The members of this order receive during life a share every day in thousands of Masses and prayers, and after death, when, alas, so many are neglected by their relatives, those who are members of this Third Order have a share daily in thousands of other Masses and prayers, this for as long as they remain in Purgatory!

Among the many beautiful characteristics of the Order of St. Dominic is its intense devotion and love for the Holy Souls, especially for the souls of its members, friends and benefactors. So true is this that a young Italian nobleman who consulted the Pope as to which religious order he would do well to enter received for answer: "My dear son, you may with much profit join any of the Orders, for in each you will find abundant means of becoming a Saint. After death, however, be a Dominican" The Holy Father meant to imply that the suffrages given after death to their deceased members are, indeed, most abundant in the Dominican Order.

The conditions of becoming a member of this order are so easy and the advantages so many that half the world would become Dominican Tertiaries did they know these advantages.

Those Who Earnestly Help the Holy Souls May Well Hope to Avoid Purgatory

The Holy Souls whom we relieve or release by our Masses and good works pray for us with such indescribable fervour that God cannot refuse to hear their prayers. One of the principal graces they ask for their friends is that these shall have little or no Purgatory. No one knows better than they the awful intensity of the Purgatorial flames; no one, therefore, can pray for us as they do. Let us remember that:

a) God thanks as done to Himself what we do to others. When we relieve or release any of the Holy Souls, we relieve or release, as it were, God Himself. How ready, therefore, will He not be to hear the prayers offered by these souls for us.

b) Our Blessed Lord lays down clearly the great law: "By that measure by which you measure, it will be measured to you again" In proportion, consequently, to our generosity towards the Holy Souls will God's mercy and generosity be towards us. Those who work heart and soul for the relief of the Holy Souls may thus well hope that their Purgatory will be entirely remitted, or notably lessened. On the other hand, those who neglect the Holy Souls may justly fear a severe judgment and a long Purgatory.

Resolution: Let everyone without fail join the Association of the Holy Souls. All the members of the family should do so. The conditions are very easy.

St. James the Apostle gives another very effectual method of avoiding or lessening our stay in Purgatory. He says: "He who saves a soul, saves his own, and satisfies for a multitude of sins"

If someone were fortunate enough to save the life of a King's only son, the heir to his throne, from a horrible death, what reward might he not expect to receive from the grateful monarch? No King, however, could be as grateful to and anxious to reward the person who saved his son as God is grateful and ready to reward the person who saves one soul from Hell.

All of us may, in a thousand different ways, save not one but many souls from Hell. For instance:

1. We can do so by praying earnestly for them. How often does not a mother save her son's soul by her fervent prayers. We can save souls by giving good advice and also by our good example. How many boys owe their sterling qualities to the wise counsels of a good Father or friend!

2. Another efficacious method of saving souls is by propagating the Faith, viz., Catholic Action.

The incredible ignorance, apathy and indifference of Catholics is the evil of the day!

It is the bounden duty of Catholics to spread about thousands and thousands of pamphlets of all kinds, full of life, vigour and burning interest, crisp, incisive, clear and strong. Otherwise, these are useless.

Each pamphlet or leaflet must carry a message straight to the heart of the reader, rousing him, convincing him, galvanizing him into action.

To Avoid Purgatory, Do As Follows

1. In every prayer you say, every Mass you hear, every Communion you receive, every good work you perform, have the express intention of imploring God to grant you a holy and happy death and no Purgatory. Surely God will hear a prayer said with such confidence and perseverance.

2. Always wish to do God's will. It is in every sense the best for you. When you do or seek anything that is not God's will, you are sure to suffer. Say fervently, therefore, each time you recite the Our Father: "Thy will be done"

3. Accept all the sufferings, sorrows, pains and disappointments of life, be they great or small: ill health, loss of goods, the death of your dear ones, heat or cold, rain or sunshine, as coming from God. Bear them calmly and patiently for love of Him

and in penance for your sins. Of course one may use all his efforts to ward off trouble and pain, but when one cannot avoid them let him bear them manfully. Impatience and revolt make sufferings vastly greater and more difficult to bear.

4. Christ's life and actions are so many lessons for us to imitate. The greatest act in His life was His Passion. As He had a Passion, so each one of us has a passion. Our passion consists in the sufferings and labors of every day. The penance God imposed on man for sin was to gain his bread with the sweat of his brow. Therefore, let us do our work, accept its disappointments and hardships, and bear our pains in union with the Passion of Christ. We gain more merit by a little pain than by years of pleasure.

5. Forgive all injuries and offences, for in proportion as we forgive others, God forgives us.

6. Avoid mortal sins and deliberate venial sins and break off all bad habits. Then it will be relatively easy to satisfy God's justice for sins of frailty. Above all, avoid sins against charity and against chastity, whether in thought, word or deed, for these sins [and the expiation for them] are the reason why many souls are detained in Purgatory for long years.

7. If afraid of doing much, do many little things, acts of kindness and charity, give the alms you can, cultivate regularity of life, method in work, and punctuality in the performance of duty; don't grumble or complain when things are not as you please; don't censure and complain of others; never refuse to do a favour to others when it is possible. These and suchlike little acts are a splendid penance.

8. Do all in your power for the Holy Souls in Purgatory. Pray for them constantly, get others to do so, join the Association of the Holy Souls and ask all those you know to do likewise. The Holy Souls will repay you most generously.

9. There is no way more powerful of obtaining from God a most holy and happy death than by weekly Confession, daily Mass and daily Communion.

10. A daily visit to the Blessed Sacrament--it need only be three or four minutes--is an easy way of obtaining the same grace. Kneeling in the presence of Jesus with eyes fixed on the Tabernacle,

sure that He is looking at us, let us for a few minutes repeat some little prayer like these:

"My Jesus, mercy."
"My Jesus, have pity on me, a sinner"
"My Jesus, I love You"
"My Jesus, give me a happy death"

Heroic Act of Charity

A good way to avoid Purgatory is to make the Heroic act of charity. Although a form of oblation is given below, all that is required is the act of the will to make the heroic act of charity.

This heroic act of charity in behalf of the Souls in Purgatory consists in the voluntary offering made for their relief, of all our works of satisfaction during life, as well as of all suffrages which may be offered for us after death. This offering we place in the hands of the Blessed Virgin Mary, that she may distribute its merits to those holy Souls whom it is her good pleasure to deliver from the pains of Purgatory.

Let it be understood, however, that we offer hereby only the special and personal portion of the satisfactory merit of our good works, so that we are not prevented from offering our good works, prayers, the Holy Sacrifice of Mass, etc., for other intentions. It is also to be remembered that, though this act is sometimes called a vow, yet it induces no obligation binding under sin.

The following indulgences were granted to those who make this heroic offering: Pope Benedict XIII., Aug. 23, 1728, made the first grant of indulgences for this act. Pius VI, Dec. 12, 1788, afterwards confirmed it, and Pius IX. again renewed and specified the indulgences in a decree dated September 30, 1852, November 20, 1854; Pius X., Feb. 20, 1907.

I. All priests who take this vow, have the indult of a privileged altar, personally, every day of the year, at whatever altar they celebrate Mass for the faithful departed.

II. All the faithful who have made this obligation, can gain a Plenary Indulgence, applicable only to the Souls in Purgatory, every time they receive Holy Communion, provided they visit a church or public oratory and pray according to the intention of His Holiness.

III. All the faithful, who have made this obligation, can apply a Plenary Indulgence to the faithful departed every Monday, by hearing Mass for this intention, provided they go to Holy Communion and visit some church and pray to the intention of the Sovereign Pontiff.

IV. All indulgences granted, or to be granted, even though not stated as applicable to the departed when gained by those who have made this obligation, can be applied to the Souls in Purgatory.

V. For those whose duties prevent their hearing Mass on Monday, the Mass heard on Sunday is sufficient to gain the Indulgence No. III.

For those who do not yet approach the holy table, or who are unable to receive Holy Communion, some other good work may be appointed by confessors, authorized by their respective bishops, to gain the Plenary Indulgence as above.

Form of Oblation

O eternal and most merciful Father, accept the oblation which I make to Thee, in union with the Most Sacred Heart of Thy Divine Son Jesus, of all the merits of the life, sufferings, and death of the same Jesus, our Lord and Savior, in behalf of the Souls, suffering in Purgatory. I offer to Thee, O Heavenly Father, for their deliverance from suffering, for their admission to the joys of Heaven, the infinite merits of the Sacred Heart of Jesus, the immense and superabundant merits of the ever-blessed Virgin Mary, of all the holy Martyrs, and of all the Saints in Heaven and on earth.

I offer, also, and resign entirely, in favor of those suffering Souls, all my satisfactory works, and those of others applied to me in life or death, and after my passage to eternity; and in order to render this poor offering of mine more acceptable to Thee, and more beneficial to the Souls for whom I make it, I unite it to the infinte and most pleasing homage which the Divine Heart of Jesus is continually paying to Thy Majesty. I place it in the most pure hands of Mary Immaculate, that she may present it to Thee, as a pleasing holocaust, and distribute according to her good pleasure the graces, favors and relief obtained from Thy infinite mercy.

Devotions For the Relief of the Poor Suffering Souls in Purgatory

Pious Catholic perform various devotions for the Poor Souls in Purgatory. For instance, there is a plenary indulgence that can be gained on All Souls Day and the seven days following by visiting a cemetery and praying for the Poor Souls. Prayer books contain many simple prayers and devotions and there is not space here to reproduce them all. Here we have reproduced three important devotions.

The first is the Office of the Dead from the Divine Office of the Church. The Divine Office or Breviary is the official prayer of the Church along side the Holy Sacrifice of the Mass. In the early centuries the Faithful would begin their observance of the Lord's day the evening before by chanting psalms and listening to readings from Sacred Scripture and hearing sermons. Their prayer would continue until morning, when the Mass was sung. From this practice the Divine Office evolved, when this was carried on by the monks and nuns in monasteries. The Mass can be considered a diamond and the Divine Office is the setting or ring and other precious stones surrounding the Mass.

Some pious souls make a Daily Pilgrimage to Purgatory every night. Special prayers have been written for this purpose, but any prayers could be attached to our night prayers before we go off silently to sleep.

The day someone dies we should commence the Novena for the Relief of the Suffering Souls in Purgatory for the repose of their souls. And what a wonderful practice it would be to ask all attending the Rosary and Funeral to take up this practice for the Poor Souls. Of course, this Novena can also be recited at any time by the faithful.

Let us add daily devotions for the relief of the poor suffering souls in Purgatory to our standard devotions.

Office of the Dead

The following Office of the Dead should be said at the time of burial by the clergy. The Faithful can say this Office at any time for a specific soul or for the Poor Souls in general. Matins and Lauds are said together in the morning. The clergy celebrate Matins and Lauds of the Dead after Matins and Lauds of the day in the Breviary. Vespers is said in the evening before dinner time.

Matins

Invitatory

The King, for whom all things live, * O come, let us worship.
The King, for whom all things live, * O come, let us worship.
Psalm 94: O come, let us sing unto the Lord; let us heartily rejoice in the God of our salvation. Let us come before his presence with thanksgiving; and shew ourselves glad in him with psalms.
The King, for whom all things live, * O come, let us worship.
For the Lord is a great God; and a great King above all gods: For the Lord will not cast off his people: In his hand are all the corners of the earth, and the strength of the hills is his also.
O come, let us worship.
The sea is his and he made it; and his hands prepared the dry land. O come, let us worship and fall down, and kneel before the Lord our Maker: For he is the Lord our God; and we are his people, and the sheep of his pasture.
The King, for whom all things live, * O come, let us worship.
Today if ye will hear his voice, harden not your hearts, as in the provocation, and as in the day of temptation in the wilderness; when your fathers tempted me, proved me, and saw my works.
O come, let us worship.
Forty years long was I grieved with this generation, and said, It is a people that do err in their hearts, for they have not known my ways: unto whom I sware in my wrath, that they should not enter into my rest.
The King, for whom all things live, * O come, let us worship.

Eternal rest grant unto them, O Lord: and let perpetual light shine upon them.
O come, let us worship.
The King, for whom all things live, * O come, let us worship.

Nocturn on Sunday, Monday and Thursday

Ant. Make my way * straight before thy face, O Lord my God.
Psalm 5. Verba mea
Ponder my words, O Lord, * consider my cry.
2 O hearken thou unto the voice of my calling, * my King and my God.
3 For unto thee will I make my prayer: * in the morning shalt thou hear my voice, O Lord.
4 Early in the morning will I stand before thee, and will see: * for thou art the God that hast no pleasure in wickedness.
5 Neither shall any evil dwell with thee: * nor shall the unjust abide before thine eyes.
6 For thou hatest all them that work iniquity: * thou shalt destroy them that speak lies.
7 The Lord will abhor both the blood-thirsty and deceitful man: * but as for me, in the multitude of thy mercy.
8 I will come into thine house; * and in thy fear will I worship toward thy holy temple.
9 Lead me, O Lord, in thy righteousness, * because of mine enemies make my way plain before thy face.
10 For there is no faithfulness in their mouth; * their heart is vain.
11 Their throat is an open sepulchre, they flatter with their tongue: * judge thou them, O God.
12 Let them perish through their own imaginations; cast them out in the multitude of their ungodliness; * for they have rebelled against thee, O Lord.
13 And let all them that put their trust in thee rejoice: * they shall for ever be glad, and thou shalt dwell amongst them.
14 And all they that love thy Name shall be joyful in thee; * for thou, Lord, wilt give thy blessing unto the righteous.

15   Thou hast crowned us, O Lord, * as with a shield of thy good will.

16 Eternal rest * grant unto them, O Lord.

17 And let perpetual light * shine upon them.

Ant.   Make my way straight before thy face, O Lord my God.

Ant.   Turn thee, * O Lord, and deliver my soul: for in death no man remembereth thee.

Psalm 6. Domine, ne in furore

O Lord, rebuke me not in thine indignation, * neither chasten me in thy displeasure.

2 Have mercy upon me, O Lord, for I am weak; * O Lord, heal me, for my bones are vexed.

3 My soul also is sore troubled: * but, thou, O Lord, how long?

4 Turn thee, O Lord, and deliver my soul; * O save me, for thy mercy's sake.

5 For in death no man remembereth thee; * and who will give thee thanks in the pit?

6 I have laboured in my groanings, every night wash I my bed, * and water my couch with my tears.

7 Mine eye is grieved with tribulation, * I have grown old amongst all mine enemies.

8 Depart from me, all ye workers of iniquity; * for the Lord hath heard the voice of my weeping.

9 The Lord hath heard my petition; * the Lord hath received my prayer.

10 All mine enemies shall be confounded, and sore vexed; * they shall be turned back, and put to shame suddenly.

11 Eternal rest * grant unto them, O Lord.

12 And let perpetual light * shine upon them

Ant.   Turn thee, O Lord, and deliver my soul: for in death no man remembereth thee.

Ant.   Lest he tear my soul * like a lion, while there is none to deliver, or to save.

Psalm 7. i. Domine, Deus meus

O Lord my God, in thee have I put my trust: * save me from all them that persecute me, and deliver me;

2 Lest he devour my soul like a lion, * while there is none to redeem me, nor to save.

3 O Lord my God, if I have done any such thing; * or if there be any wickedness in my hands;

4 If I have rewarded evil unto him that dealt friendly with me; * let me deservedly fall empty before mine enemies.

5 Then let mine enemy persecute my soul, yea, let him take it, and tread my life down upon the earth, * and lay mine honour in the dust.

6 Arise, O Lord, in thy wrath, * and be thou exalted in the land of mine enemies.

7 And rise up, O Lord my God, in the judgment that thou hast commanded; * and so shall the congregation of the people come about thee.

8 For their sakes therefore lift up thyself again on high, * the Lord judgeth the people.

9 Give sentence with me, O Lord, according to my righteousness, * and according to the innocence that is in me.

10 The wickedness of the ungodly shall be brought to nought, and thou shalt guide the just, * for God is the searcher of the hearts and reins.

11 My help is just that cometh of the Lord, * who saveth them that are true of heart.

12 God is a righteous Judge, strong, and patient; * and shall he be provoked every day?

13 If a man will not turn, he will whet his sword; * he hath bent his bow, and made it ready.

14 He hath prepared for him the instruments of death; * he hath ordained his arrows against them that burn.

15 Behold, he travaileth with injustice; * he hath conceived sorrow, and brought forth ungodliness.

16 He hath graven and digged up a pit, * and is fallen himself into the hole that he hath made.

17 For his sorrow shall come upon his own head, * and his wickedness shall fall on his own pate.

18 I will give thanks unto the Lord, according to his righteousness; * and I will praise the Name of the Lord Most High.

19 Eternal rest * grant unto them, O Lord.

20 And let perpetual light * shine upon them.

Ant. Lest he tear my soul like a lion, while there is none to deliver, or to save.

V. From the gates of hell.

R. Deliver their souls, O Lord.

Our Father, of which nothing is said aloud

Lesson 1

Spare me, O Lord, for my days are as a breath. What is man, that thou shouldest magnify him? and that thou shouldest set thine heart upon him? And that thou shouldest visit him every morning, and try him every moment? How long wilt thou refuse me respite from thy visitation, and suffer me not even to swallow down my spittle? If I have sinned, what can I do unto thee, O thou Watcher of men? why hast thou set me over against thee as a mark for thy buffetings, so that I am a burden to myself? And why dost thou not pardon my transgression, and take away mine iniquity? for soon shall I sleep in the dust; and if then thou dost seek for me, I shall not be.

R. I know that my Redeemer liveth, and that he shall stand in the latter day upon the earth, * And in my flesh shall I see God my Saviour.

V. Whom I shall see for myself, and mine eyes shall behold, and not as a stranger.

R. And in my flesh shall I see God my Saviour.

Lesson 2

My soul is weary of my life: I will give free course to my complaint; I will speak in the bitterness of my soul. I will say unto God: Do not condemn me; shew me wherefore thou judgest me thus. Doth it seem good to thee that thou shouldest maltreat me, that thou shouldest despise the work of thine hands, and shine upon the counsel of the wicked? Hast thou eyes of flesh? or seest thou as man seeth? are thy days as the days of man? are thy years as the times of man, that thou inquirest after mine iniquity, and searchest after my sin? Yet thou knowest that I have done no wrong, and that there is none that can deliver out of thine hand.

R. Thou that didst raise Lazarus from the grave after that he had begun to corrupt, * Do thou, O Lord, grant them rest and a place of forgiveness.

V. Thou who shalt come to judge the quick and the dead, and the world by fire.

R. Do thou, O Lord, grant them rest and a place of forgiveness.

Lesson 3

Thine hands have made me and fashioned me together round about; and yet wouldest thou so suddenly destroy me? Remember, I beseech thee, that thou hast made me as the clay, and that thou wilt bring me into the dust again. Hast thou not poured me out as milk, and curdled me like cheese? Thou hast clothed me with skin and flesh, and hast knit me together with bones and sinews. Thou hast granted me life and mercy, and thy visitation hath preserved my spirit.

R. O Lord, when thou comest to judge the earth, whither shall I hide me from the presence of thy wrath? * For I have sinned grievously in my life.

V. I begin to fear my misdeeds, and blush before thee: when thou comest to judgment, condemn me not.

R. For I have sinned grievously in my life.

V. Eternal rest grant unto them, O Lord, and let perpetual light shine upon them.

R. For I have sinned grievously in my life.

Proceed to Lauds, which should be joined to Matins.

Nocturn For Tuesday and Friday

Psalm 22. Dominus regit me

Ant. In a green pasture * he shall feed me.

The Lord is my shepherd, and I shall want nothing: * he hath set me in a green pasture.

2 He hath led me forth beside the waters of comfort: * he hath converted my soul.

3 He hath brought me forth in the paths of righteousness * for his Name's sake.

4 Yea, though I walk through the valley of the shadow of death, I will fear no evil; * for thou art with me.

5 Thy rod and thy staff, * they have comforted me.

6 Thou hast prepared a table before me * in the presence of them that trouble me.

7 Thou hast anointed my head with oil: * and my cup which inebriateth me, how goodly it is.

8 And thy mercy shall follow me * all the days of my life.

9 And I will dwell in the house of the Lord * unto length of days.

10 Eternal rest * grant unto them, O Lord.

11 And let perpetual light * shine upon them.

Ant.   In a green pasture he shall feed me.

Ant.   O remember not * the sins and offences of my youth.

Psalm 24. Ad te Domine

Unto thee, O Lord, have I lifted up my soul: * my God, in thee do I trust, O let me not be confounded.

2 Neither let mine enemies triumph over me: * for all they that hope in thee shall not be confounded.

3 Let all be put to confusion such as transgress * without a cause.

4 Shew me thy ways, O Lord, * and teach me thy paths.

5 Lead me forth in thy truth, and teach me: * for thou art my Saviour, O God, and in thee hath been my hope all the day long.

6 Call to remembrance, O Lord, thy tender mercies, * and thy loving-kindnesses, which have been ever of old.

7 O remember not * the sins and offences of my youth.

8 But according to thy mercy think thou upon me, * for the sake of thy goodness, O Lord.

9 Gracious and righteous is the Lord; * therefore, will he give a law unto them that sin in the way.

10 Them that are meek shall he guide in judgment; * and such as are gentle, them shall he teach his way.

11 All the paths of the Lord are mercy and truth, * unto such as seek after his covenant and his testimonies.

12 For thy Name's sake, O Lord, be merciful unto my sin; * for it is great.

13 What man is he that feareth the Lord? * him hath he appointed a law in the way that he hath chosen.

14 His soul shall dwell at ease, * and his seed shall inherit the land.

15 The Lord is a firmament among them that fear him; * and he will shew them his covenant.

16 Mine eyes are ever looking unto the Lord; * for he shall pluck my feet out of the net.

17 Turn thee unto me, and have mercy upon me; * for I am alone and in need.

18 The sorrows of my heart are enlarged: * O bring thou me out of my necessities.

19 Look upon my abjection and my labour, * and forgive me all my sin.

20 Consider mine enemies, for they are multiplied: * and have hated me with a tyrannous hatred.

21 O keep my soul, and deliver me: * let me not be confounded, for I have put my trust in thee.

22 The innocent and the righteous have adhered unto me; * for my hope hath been in thee.

23 Deliver Israel, O God, * out of all his troubles.

24 Eternal rest * grant unto them, O Lord.

25 And let perpetual light * shine upon them.

Ant. O remember not * the sins and offences of my youth.

Ant. I believe verily to see the goodness of the Lord in the land of the living.

Psalm 26. Dominus illuminatio mea

The Lord is my light and my salvation; * whom then shall I fear?

2 The Lord is the protector of my life; * of whom then shall I be afraid?

3 When the wicked draw nigh against me, * to eat up my flesh,

4 Even mine enemies that trouble me, * have themselves been weakened and have fallen.

5 Though an host of men were laid against me, * yet shall not my heart be afraid.

6 And though a battle should rise up against me, * yet will I put my trust in him.

7 One thing have I desired of the Lord, which I will require; * even that I may dwell in the house of the Lord all the days of my life,

8 To behold the fair beauty of the Lord, * and to visit his temple.

9 For he hath hidden me in his tabernacle; * in the day of evils, yea, he hath protected me in the secret place of his dwelling.

10 He hath set me up upon a rock of stone: * and now he hath lifted up mine head above mine enemies.

11 I have gone round about, and have offered a sacrifice of jubilation in his dwelling: * I will sing and speak praises unto the Lord.

12 Hearken unto my voice, O Lord, when I cry unto thee; * have mercy upon me, and hear me.

13 My heart hath said unto thee, My face hath sought thee: * thy face, Lord, will I seek.

14 O hide not thou thy face from me, * nor cast thy servant away in displeasure.

15 Thou hast been my succour; * leave me not, neither forsake me, O God of my salvation.

16 For my father and my mother have forsaken me, * but the Lord hath taken me up.

17 Set me a law in thy way, O Lord, * and lead me in the right way, because of mine enemies.

18 Deliver me not over into the will of mine adversaries: * for there are false witnesses risen up against me, and wickedness hath lied to itself.

19 I believe verily to see the goodness of the Lord * in the land of the living.

20 Expect thou the Lord and act manfully; * and thine heart shall be comforted; and wait thou for the Lord.

21 Eternal rest * grant unto them, O Lord.

22 And let perpetual light * shine upon them.

Ant. I believe verily to see the goodness of the Lord in the land of the living.

V. May the Lord set them with the princes.
R. Even with the princes of his people.
Our Father, of which nothing is said aloud.

Lesson 1

Answer thou me: How many are mine iniquities and misdeeds? make me to know my transgressions and offences. Wherefore hidest thou thy face, and holdest me for thine enemy? Dost thou shew forth thy power against a leaf driven to and fro by the wind? And wilt thou pursue the dry stubble? For thou writest bitter things against me, and makest me to inherit the iniquities of my youth. Thou puttest my feet in the stocks, and lookest narrowly unto all my paths; thou observest my footsteps, even though I am to waste away as a rotten thing, and as a garment that is moth-eaten.

R. O remember, Lord God, that my life is a breath! * Soon the eye of him that seeth me shall behold me no more.

V. Out of the deep have I called unto thee, O Lord: Lord, hear my voice.

R. Soon the eye of him that seeth me shall behold me no more.

Lesson 2

Man that is born of a woman hath but a short time to live, and is full of misery. He cometh forth like a flower, and is cut down; he fleeth as it were a shadow, and feeth as a shadow. And dost thou think it worthy to open thine eyes upon such an one, and to bring him into judgment with thee? Who can bring a clean thing out of an unclean? Is it not thou who alone art? The days of man are short, and the number of his months is with thee; thou hast appointed his bounds that he cannot pass. Turn from him for a little while, that he may rest, till he shall accomplish, as an hireling, his day.

R. Woe is me, O Lord, for I have grievously sinned in my life! What shall I do, wretched man that I am? Whither shall I flee, but unto thee, my God? * Have mercy upon me, when thou comest at the last day.

V. My soul is sore troubled; but, Lord, be thou my helper.

R. Have mercy upon me, when thou comest at the last day.

Lesson 3

O that thou wouldest hide me in the grave; that thou wouldest keep me secret, until thy wrath be past; that thou wouldest appoint me a set time, and remember me! If a man die, thinkest thou that he shall live again? All the days wherein I now toil, I will wait till my release come. Then thou shalt call, and I will answer thee: thou wilt stretch forth thy right hand unto the work of thine hands. Thou dost indeed number my steps, but be thou merciful unto my sins.

R. Remember not my sins, O Lord, * When thou shalt come to judge the world by fire.

V. Make thy way plain, O Lord my God, before my face.

R. When thou shalt come to judge the world by fire.

V. Eternal rest grant unto them, O Lord, and let perpetual light shine upon them.

R. When thou shalt come to judge the world by fire.

Go to Lauds

Nocturn For Wednesday and Saturday

Ant. Let it be thy pleasure * to deliver me, O Lord: make haste, O Lord, to help me.

Psalm 39. Exspectans exspectavi

With expectation I have waited for the Lord, * and he inclined unto me.

2 And he heard my prayers: * and he brought me also out of the horrible pit, out of the mire and clay.

3 And he hath set my feet upon the rock, * and ordered my goings.

4 And he hath put a new canticle in my mouth, * even a song unto our God.

5 Many shall see it, and fear, * and shall put their trust in the Lord.

6 Blessed is the man that hath set his hope in the Name of the Lord, * and who hath not turned unto vanity, and to lying follies.

7 O Lord my God, great are the wondrous works which thou hast done, * and in thy thoughts there is no one like unto thee.

8 I have declared and I have spoken: * they are multiplied above number.

9 Sacrifice and offering thou wouldest not, * but mine ears hast thou opened.

10 Burnt-offering and sacrifice for sin hast thou not required: * then said I, Lo, I come;

11 In the volume of the book it is written of me, that I should fulfil thy will, * O my God, I am content to do it; yea, thy law is within my heart.

12 I have declared thy righteousness in the great congregation: * lo, I will not refrain my lips, O Lord, and that thou knowest.

13 I have not hid thy righteousness within my heart; * I have declared thy truth and thy salvation.

14 I have not concealed thy loving mercy and truth * from the great congregation.

15 Withdraw not thou thy mercy from me, O Lord; * thy loving-kindness and thy truth have ever preserved me.

16 For evils without number are come about me; * my sins have taken such hold upon me, that I am not able to look up.

17 Yea, they are more in number than the hairs of my head, and my heart hath failed me.

18 O Lord, let it be thy pleasure to deliver me; * make haste, O Lord, to help me.

19 Let them be ashamed, and confounded together, that seek after my soul * to destroy it.

20 Let them be driven backward, and put to rebuke, * that wish me evil.

21 Let them immediately be rewarded with shame: * that say unto me, Fie upon thee! fie upon thee!

22 Let all those that seek thee rejoice and be glad in thee; * and let such as love thy salvation, say alway, The Lord be magnified.

23 As for me, I am poor and needy; * but the Lord careth for me.

24 Thou art my helper and protector; * make no long tarrying, O my God.

25 Eternal rest * grant unto them, O Lord.

26 And let perpetual light * shine upon them.

Ant.   Let it be thy pleasure to deliver me, O Lord: make haste, O Lord, to help me.

Ant.   Heal my soul, * O Lord, for I have sinned against thee.

Psalm 40. Beatus qui intelligit

Blessed is he that considereth the poor and needy; * the Lord shall deliver him in the time of trouble.

2 The Lord preserve him, and give him life, and make him blessed upon earth; * and deliver him not up into the will of his enemies.

3 The Lord comfort him upon his bed of sorrows; * thou hast turned all his couch in his sickness.

4 I said, Lord, be merciful unto me; * heal my soul, for I have sinned against thee.

5 Mine enemies have spoken evil of me, * When shall he die, and his name perish?

6 And if he came to see me, he spake vanity, * and his heart conceived falsehood within itself.

7 He went forth, * and spake in the selfsame.

8 All mine enemies whispered together against me; * against me did they imagine evils.

9 They established an evil word against me: * Shall he that sleepeth rise again no more?

10 Yea, even the man of my peace, in whom I trusted, * who did also eat of my bread, hath laid great wait for me.

11 But be thou merciful unto me, O Lord, and raise thou me up again, * and I shall reward them.

12 By this I know thou hast favoured me, * for mine enemy shall not triumph against me.

13 And because of my innocence thou upholdest me, * and shalt set me before thy face for ever.

14 Blessed be the Lord God of Israel, for ever and ever, and world without end: * Amen, Amen.

15 Eternal rest * grant unto them, O Lord.

16 And let perpetual light * shine upon them.

Ant.   Heal my soul, O Lord, for I have sinned against thee.

Ant. My soul is athirst * for God, yea, even for the living God: when shall I come to appear before the presence of God?

Psalm 41. Quemadmodum

Like as the hart desireth the water-brooks, * so longeth my soul after thee, O God.

2 My soul is athirst for God, yea, even for the strong, living God: * when shall I come to appear before the presence of God?

3 My tears have been my meat day and night, * while they daily say unto me, Where is now thy God?

4 These things I remembered, and poured out my soul within me; * for I shall go over into the place of the wondrous tabernacle, even unto the house of God.

5 In the voice of praise and thanksgiving, * the sound of one keeping holy-day.

6 Why art thou sad, O my soul? * and why dost thou trouble me?

7 O put thy trust in God, for I will yet praise him, * the salvation of my countenance, and my God.

8 My soul is vexed within me; * therefore will I remember thee from the land of Jordan, from Hermon and the little hill.

9 The deep calleth on the deep, * at the noise of thy water-floods.

10 All thy waves and storms * are gone over me.

11 The Lord hath commanded his mercy in the daytime; * and a canticle to him in the night season.

12 The prayer to the God of my life is with me, * I will say unto God: Thou dost uphold me.

13 Why hast thou forgotten me? * and why go I mourning, whilst the enemy oppresseth me?

14 Whilst my bones are smitten asunder, * mine enemies that trouble me have reproached me.

15 While they say daily unto me: Where is now thy God? * why art thou sad, O my soul? and why dost thou trouble me?

16 O put thy trust in God, for I will yet praise him, * the salvation of my countenance, and my God.

17 Eternal rest * grant unto them, O Lord.

18 And let perpetual light * shine upon them.

Ant.   My soul is athirst for God, yea, even for the living God: when shall I come to appear before the presence of God?

V.   Deliver not up unto the beasts the souls of them that praise thee.

R. And forget not the congregation of the poor for ever.

Our Father, of which nothing is said aloud.

Lesson 1

My breath will wax feebler, and my days fewer, and there is nothing before me but the grave. I have not sinned; yet my mind remaineth in affliction. Deliver me, O Lord, and set me beside thee; and let not any man's hand fight against me. My days are past, my purposes are broken off, and are but vexation to my spirit. They change the night into day, and again, after the darkness I hope for light. If I wait, the grave is mine house; I have made my bed in the darkness. I have said to corruption: thou art my father; to the worm: thou art my mother, and my sister. Where therefore is now my hope? As for my patience, who shall consider it?

R. It is upon such an one as myself, who doth sin often and repent seldom, and then but little, that the fear of death befalleth: * Because in hell there is no redemption, have mercy upon me, O God, and save me.

V. Save me, O God, for thy Name's sake, and deliver me in thy strength.

R. Because in hell there is no redemption, have mercy upon me, O God, and save me.

Lesson 2

My flesh is consumed, my bone cleaveth unto my skin, and there remaineth not round my teeth save the skin of my lips. Have pity upon me, have pity upon me , at least ye that are my friends, for the hand of the Lord hath touched me. Why do ye persecute me as doth God, and glut yourselves upon my flesh? O that my words were now written! O that they were inscribed in a book with an iron pen, or cut in lead, or graven with a chisel upon the flinty rock! For I know that my Redeemer liveth, and that I shall stand up from the earth at the latter day, and in my flesh shall I see God; whom I shall see for myself, and mine eyes shall behold, and not another. This is mine hope that is laid up in my bosom.

R. O Lord, judge me not according to my deeds, for nothing have I done that is worthy in thy sight; therefore do I come before thy Majesty as a suppliant; * That thou, O God, mayest blot out mine iniquity.

V. Wash me throughly from my wickedness, and cleanse me from my sin.

R. That thou, O God, mayest blot out mine iniquity.

Lesson 3

Wherefore then hast thou brought me forth out of the womb? O that I had given up the ghost, and no eye had seen me! I should have been as though I had not been; I should have been carried from the womb to the grave. Are not my days few? Let me alone then, that I may comfort myself a little in my sorrow, before I go whence I shall not return, even to the land of darkness and the shadow of death, the land of misery and darkness, where the night of death dwelleth, without any order, but shapelessness and dreadfulness of darkness for ever.

R. Deliver me, O Lord, from the paths of hell, even thou that didst break the gates of brass; even thou that didst visit hell, and gavest light to the inhabitants thereof, that they might see thee: * Them that were in the pains of darkness.

V. Them that were crying aloud and saying: Thou hast come, O our Redeemer.

R. Them that were in the pains of darkness.

V. Eternal rest grant unto them, O Lord: and let perpetual light shine upon them.

R. Them that were in the pains of darkness.
Go to Lauds

The following Responsory is said in place of the preceding, when all three Nocturns for the Dead have been said at Matins.

R. Deliver me, O Lord, from everlasting death in that fearful day: * When the heavens and the earth shall be shaken: * When thou shalt come to judge the world by fire.

V. I am in fear and trembling, until the sifting be upon us and the wrath to come.

R. When the heavens and the earth shall be shaken.

V. Woe is me, for the day of wrath, calamity and misery, the great day of exceeding bitterness.

R. When thou shalt come to judge the world by fire.

V. Eternal rest grant unto them, O Lord, and let perpetual light shine upon them.

R. Deliver me, O Lord, from everlasting death in that fearful day: * When the heavens and the earth shall be shaken: * When thou shalt come to judge the world by fire.

Lauds of the Dead

Ant. The bones which thou hast broken * shall rejoice in the Lord

Psalm 50. Miserere mei, Deus

Have mercy upon me, O God, * after thy great goodness.

2 According to the multitude of thy mercies * do away mine offences.

3 Wash me throughly from my wickedness, * and cleanse me from my sin.

4 For I acknowledge my faults, * and my sin is ever before me.

5 Against thee only have I sinned, and done this evil in thy sight; * that thou mightest be justified in thy saying, and clear when thou art judged.

6 Behold, I was shapen in wickedness, * and in sin hath my mother conceived me.

7 But lo, thou requirest truth in the inward parts, * and shalt make me to understand wisdom secretly.

8 Thou shalt purge me with hyssop, and I shall be clean; * thou shalt wash me, and I shall be whiter than snow.

9 Thou shalt make me hear of joy and gladness, * that the bones which thou hast broken may rejoice.

10 Turn thy face from my sins, * and put out all my misdeeds.

11 Make me a clean heart, O God, * and renew a right spirit within me.

12 Cast me not away from thy presence, * and take not thy holy Spirit from me.

13 O give me the comfort of thy help again, * and establish me with thy free Spirit.

14 Then shall I teach thy ways unto the wicked, * and sinners shall be converted unto thee.

15 Deliver me from blood-guiltiness, O God, thou that art the God of my health; * and my tongue shall sing of thy righteousness.

16 Thou shalt open my lips, O Lord, * and my mouth shall shew thy praise.

17 For thou desirest no sacrifice, else would I give it thee; * but thou delightest not in burnt-offerings.

18 The sacrifice of God is a troubled spirit: * a broken and contrite heart, O God, shalt thou not despise.

19 O be favourable and gracious unto Sion; * build thou the walls of Jerusalem.

20 Then shalt thou be pleased with the sacrifice of righteousness, with the burnt-offerings and oblations; * then shall they offer young bullocks upon thine altar.

21 Eternal rest * grant unto them, O Lord.

22 And let perpetual light * shine upon them.

Ant. The bones which thou hast broken shall rejoice in the Lord

Ant. O Lord, hear my prayer; * unto thee shall all flesh come.

Psalm 64. Te decet hymnus

Thou art worthy to be praised, O God, in Sion; * and a vow shall be paid thee in Jerusalem.

2 O hear thou my prayer, * unto thee shall all flesh come.

3 The words of the wicked have prevailed against us: * and thou shalt pardon our transgressions.

4 Blessed is the man whom thou hast chosen and taken unto thee: * in thy courts shall he dwell.

5 We shall be filled with the good things of thy house, holy is thy temple: * wonderful in thy righteousness.

6 Hear us, O God of our salvation; * thou that art the hope of all the ends of the earth, and in the broad sea.

7 Who by thy strength settest fast the mountains, and art girded about with power: * who makest the deep sea to rage, and the noise of its waves.

8 The heathen shall be thrown into confusion, and they also that dwell in the uttermost parts of the earth shall be afraid at thy signs, * thou shalt make the out-goings of the morning and evening to rejoice.

9 Thou hast visited the earth, and made it plentiful; * thou hast many ways enriched it.

10 The river of God is full of water: * thou hast prepared their food, for so is thy providence.

11 Fill up plentifully the streams thereof, increase its fruits: * it shall spring forth and rejoice in its drops of rain.

12 Thou shalt bless the crown of the year with thy goodness; * and thy fields shall be filled with plenty.

13 The beauty of the wilderness shall grow fat: * and the hills shall be girded about with joy.

14 The rams of the flock are clothed, and the vales also shall abound with corn, * they shall call out, yea, they shall sing praises.

15 Eternal rest * grant unto them, O Lord.

16 And let perpetual light * shine upon them.

Ant. O Lord, hear my prayer; unto thee shall all flesh come.

Ant. Thy right hand, * O Lord, hath upholden me.

Psalm 62. Deus, Deus meus

O God, thou art my God; * to thee do I watch at break of day.

2 My soul hath thirsted for thee, * my flesh also in many different ways.

3 In a barren and dry land where no water is: * so in the sanctuary have I come before thee, that I might behold thy power and thy glory.

4 For thy mercy is better than the life itself: * my lips shall praise thee.

5 Thus will I bless thee as long as I live: * and I will lift up my hands in thy Name.

6 My soul shall be filled as with marrow and fatness, * and my mouth shall praise thee with joyful lips.

7 If I have remembered thee in my bed, I will think upon thee in the morning: * because thou hast been my helper.

8 And under the shadow of thy wings will I rejoice, my soul hath hung upon thee; * thy right hand hath upholden me.

9 But they have sought my soul in vain, they shall go down into the nether parts of the earth: * they shall be delivered into the hands of the sword, they shall be a portion for foxes.

10 But the king shall rejoice in God; all they also that swear by him shall be commended; * for the mouth of them that speak wicked things shall be stopped.

11 Eternal rest * grant unto them, O Lord.

12 And let perpetual light * shine upon them.

Ant.   Thy right hand, O Lord, hath upholden me.

Ant.   From the portals of hell, * deliver my soul, O Lord.

Canticle of Hezekias.   Isa. 38.10.

I said, In the midst of my days * I shall go down unto the portals of hell.

2 I sought for the residue of my years. * I said, I shall not see the Lord God in the land of the living.

3 I shall behold man no more, * neither the inhabitant of the land of rest.

4 Mine age is departed, and is rolled up from me, * like as it were a shepherd's tent.

5 My life is cut off as by a weaver, whilst I was yet but beginning, he cut me off: * from morning even until night shalt thou make an end of me.

6 I hoped till morning, * as a lion, so hath he broken all my bones.

7 From morning even until night shalt thou make an end of me: * I will cry like a young swallow; I will meditate like a dove.

8 Mine eyes are weakened, * with looking upward.

9 O Lord, I suffer violence, answer thou for me. * What shall I say, or what shall he answer me, whereas he himself hath done it?

10 I will call to remembrance before thee all my years * in the bitterness of my soul.

11 O Lord, if man's life be such, and the life of my spirit be in such things as these, thou shalt chasten me, and make me to live. * Behold, in peace is my my bitterness most bitter.

12 But thou hast delivered my soul that it should not perish: * thou hast cast all my sins behind thy back.

13 For hell shall not give glory unto thee, neither shall death praise thee, * nor yet shall they that go down into the pit look for thy truth.

14 The living, yea the living, he shall give praise unto thee, as I do this day; * the father to the children shall make known thy truth.

15 O Lord, save me, * and we will sing our psalms all the days of our life in the house of the Lord.

16 Eternal rest * grant unto them, O Lord.

17 And let perpetual light * shine upon them.

Ant. From the portals of hell, deliver my soul, O Lord.

Ant. Let everything that hath breath * praise the Lord.

Psalm 150. Laudate Dominum

O praise the Lord in his sanctuary: * praise him in the firmament of his power.

2 Praise him in his mighty acts: * praise him according to the multitude of his greatness.

3 Praise him in the sound of the trumpet: * praise him upon the lute and harp.

4 Praise him in the timbrels and choir: * praise him upon the strings and organs.

5 Praise him upon the high-sounding cymbals: praise him upon the cymbals of joy: * let every spirit praise the Lord.

6 Eternal rest * grant unto them, O Lord.

7 And let perpetual light * shine upon them.

Ant. Let everything that hath breath praise the Lord.

V. I heard a voice from heaven, saying unto me.

R. Blessed are the dead, which die in the Lord.

Antinphon at the Benedictus: I am * the resurrection and the life: he that believeth in me, though he were dead, yet shall he live; and whosoever liveth and believeth in me shall never die.

THE SONG OF ZACHARIAS
Luc. 1. 68-79

Blessed † be the Lord God of Israel; * for he hath visited and redeemed his people;

2 And hath raised up a mighty salvation for us, * in the house of his servant David;

3 As he spake by the mouth of his holy Prophets, * which have been since the world began;

4 That we should be saved from our enemies, * and from the hand of all that hate us.

5 To perform the mercy promised to our forefathers, * and to remember his holy Covenant;

6 To perform the oath which he swore to our forefather Abraham, * that he would give us;

7 That we being delivered out of the hand of our enemies * might serve him without fear;

8 In holiness and righteousness before him, * all the days of our life.

9 And thou, child, shalt be called the Prophet of the Highest: * for thou shalt go before the face of the Lord to prepare his ways;

10 To give knowledge of salvation unto his people * for the remission of their sins,

11 Through the tender mercy of our God; * whereby the Day-Spring from on high hath visited us;

12 To give light to them that sit in darkness, and in the shadow of death, * and to guide our feet into the way of peace.

13 Eternal rest * grant unto them, O Lord.

14 And let perpetual light * shine upon them.

Ant: I am the resurrection and the life: he that believeth in me, though he were dead, yet shall he live; and whosoever liveth and believeth in me shall never die.

Our Father aloud, then secretly as far as:

V. And lead us not into temptation.

R. But deliver us from evil.

The following Psalm 129, De profundis, is not said on the day of death, nor on the day of burial of the deceased, nor is it said on whatsoever day the Office is recited according to the rank of Double.

Psalm 129. De profundis

Out of the depths I have cried unto thee, O Lord; * Lord, hear my voice.

2 O let thine ears be attentive * to the voice of my supplication.

3 If thou, O Lord, shalt observe our iniquities, * Lord, who may endure it?

4 For with thee there is merciful forgiveness: * and by reason of thy law, I have waited for thee, O Lord.

5 My soul hath relied on his word * my soul hath hoped in the Lord.

6 From the morning watch even until night: * let Israel hope in the Lord.

7 Because with the Lord there is mercy, * and with him plentiful redemption.

8 And he shall redeem Israel * from all his iniquities.

9 Eternal rest * grant unto them, O Lord.

10 And let perpetual light * shine upon them.

V. From the gates of hell.
R. Deliver their souls, O Lord.
V. May they rest in peace.
R. Amen.
V. O Lord, hear my prayer.
R. And let my cry come unto thee
V. The Lord be with you.
R. And with thy spirit.

Note the following prayer is said ordinarily. However, for specific intentions see the section of special prayers at the end of this chapter on the Office of the Dead. (On page 99)

Let us pray.

O God, who didst cause thy servants, for whom we pray, to enjoy the dignity of the priesthood, and some to be bishops, after the order of thine Apostles: grant unto them, we beseech thee, finally to rejoice in the company of those Saints in heaven whose ministry they did sometime share on earth.

O God, who desirest not the death of a sinner but rather that all mankind should be saved: we beseech thee mercifully to grant that the brethren, kinsfolk, and benefactors of our congregation, who have passed out of this world, may by the intercession of blessed Mary Ever-Virgin and of all thy Saints come to enjoy with them everlasting blessedness.

O God, the Creator and Redeemer of all them that believe: grant unto the souls of thy servants and handmaidens the remission of all their sins; that as they have ever desired thy merciful pardon, so by the supplications of their brethren they may receive the same.

Who livest and reignest with the Father, in the unity of the Holy Ghost, ever one God, world without end.
R. Amen.
V. Eternal rest grant unto them, O Lord.
R. And let perpetual light shine upon them.
V. May they rest in peace. R. Amen.

Vespers of the Dead

Ant. I will walk before the Lord * in the land of the living.
Psalm 114. Dilexi, quoniam
I am well pleased, because the Lord hath heard * the voice of my prayer;
2 Because he hath inclined his ear unto me; * therefore will I call upon him all my days.
3 The sorrows of death compassed me round about, * and the perils of hell grabbed hold upon me.
4 Sorrow and trouble did I find; * then called I upon the Name of the Lord.
5 O Lord, deliver my soul: * gracious is the Lord, and righteous; yea, our God is merciful.
6 The Lord preserveth the simple: * I was brought low, and he delivered me.
7 Return unto thy rest, O my soul; * for the Lord hath dealt bountifully with thee.
8 For he hath delivered my soul from death, * mine eyes from tears, and my feet from falling.
9 I will walk before the Lord * in the land of the living.
10 Eternal rest * grant unto them, O Lord.
11 And let perpetual light * shine upon them.
Ant. I will walk before the Lord in the land of the living.
Ant. Woe is me, O Lord, * that I am constrained to dwell among them that are enemies unto peace.
Psalm 119. Ad Dóminum
When I was in trouble, I called upon the Lord, * and he heard me.
2 Deliver my soul, O Lord, from lying lips, * and from a deceitful tongue.

3 What reward shall be given or done unto thee, thou false tongue? * even mighty and sharp arrows, with hot burning coals.

4 Woe is me, that I am constrained to dwell with Meshech, * and to have my habitation among the tents of Kedar!

5 My soul hath long dwelt among them * that are enemies unto peace.

6 I labour for peace; but when I speak unto them thereof, * they make them ready to battle.

7 Eternal rest * grant unto them, O Lord.

8 And let perpetual light * shine upon them.

Ant.   Woe is me, O Lord, that I am constrained to dwell among them that are enemies unto peace.

Ant.   The Lord shall preserve thee * from all evil; yea, it is even he that shall keep thy soul.

Psalm 120. Levavi oculos

I have lifted up mine eyes unto the hills; * from whence cometh my help.

2 My help cometh even from the Lord, * who hath made heaven and earth.

3 May he not suffer thy foot to be moved; * neither let him slumber that keepeth thee.

4 Behold, he that keepeth Israel * shall neither slumber nor sleep.

5 The Lord is thy keeper, the Lord is thy defence * upon thy right hand.

6 The sun shall not burn thee by day, * neither the moon by night.

7 The Lord shall preserve thee from all evil; * yea, it is even he that shall keep thy soul.

8 The Lord shall preserve thy going out, and thy coming in, * from this time forth for evermore.

9 Eternal rest * grant unto them, O Lord.

10 And let perpetual light * shine upon them.

Ant.   The Lord shall preserve thee from all evil; yea, it is even he that shall keep thy soul.

Ant.   If thou, Lord, wilt be extreme * to mark what is done amiss, O Lord, who may abide it?

Psalm 129. De profundis

Out of the depths I have cried unto thee, O Lord; * Lord, hear my voice.

2 O let thine ears be attentive * to the voice of my supplication.

3 If thou, O Lord, shalt observe our iniquities, * Lord, who may endure it?

4 For with thee there is merciful forgiveness: * and by reason of thy law, I have waited for thee, O Lord.

5 My soul hath relied on his word * my soul hath hoped in the Lord.

6 From the morning watch even until night: * let Israel hope in the Lord.

7 Because with the Lord there is mercy, * and with him plentiful redemption.

8 And he shall redeem Israel * from all his iniquities.

9 Eternal rest * grant unto them, O Lord.

10 And let perpetual light * shine upon them.

Ant.   If thou, Lord, wilt be extreme to mark what is done amiss, O Lord, who may abide it?

Ant.   Despise not, O Lord, * the works of thine own hands.

Psalm 137. Confitebor tibi

I will give thanks unto thee, O Lord, with my whole heart; * for thou hast heard the words of my mouth.

2 Even before the Angels will I sing praise unto thee, * I will worship toward thy holy temple, and I will give glory unto thy Name.

3 Because of thy loving-kindness and truth; * for thou hast magnified thy holy Name above all things.

4 In what day soever I shall call upon thee, hear thou me; * thou shalt endue my soul with much strength.

5 May all the kings of the earth give glory unto thee, O Lord; * for they have heard all the words of thy mouth.

6 Yea, they shall sing in the ways of the Lord, * for great is the glory of the Lord.

7 For the Lord is high, yet looketh he upon the lowly; * and the high he knoweth them afar off.

8 Though I walk in the midst of tribulation, yet shalt thou quicken me; * and thou hast stretched forth thy hand upon the furiousness of mine enemies, and thy right hand hath saved me.

9 The Lord shall render for me; * yea, thy mercy, O Lord, endureth for ever; despise not then the works of thine own hands.

10 Eternal rest * grant unto them, O Lord.

11 And let perpetual light * shine upon them.

Ant.   Despise not, O Lord, the works of thine own hands.

V. I heard a voice from heaven, saying unto me.

R. Blessed are the dead, which die in the Lord.

Antiphon at Magnificat: All * that the Father hath given unto me shall come unto me, and him that cometh unto me I will in no wise cast out.

CANTICLE OF THE BLESSED VIRGIN MARY

Luc. 1. 46-55

MY SOUL doth magnify the Lord, † * and my spirit hath rejoiced in God my Saviour.

2 For he hath regarded * the lowliness of his handmaiden.

3 For behold, from henceforth * all generations shall call me blessed.

4 For he that is mighty hath magnified me; * (Here all make a profound reverence) and holy is his Name.

5 And his mercy is on them that fear him * throughout all generations.

6 He hath shewed strength with his arm; * he hath scattered the proud in the imagination of their hearts.

7 He hath put down the mighty from their seat, * and hath exalted the humble and meek.

8 He hath filled the hungry with good things; * and the rich he hath sent empty away.

9 He remembering his mercy hath helped his servant Israel; * as he promised to our forefathers, Abraham and his seed for ever.

10 Eternal rest * grant unto them, O Lord.

11 And let perpetual light * shine upon them.

Ant: All that the Father hath given unto me shall come unto me, and him that cometh unto me I will in no wise cast out.

Our Father aloud, then secretly as far as:

V. And lead us not into temptation.

R. But deliver us from evil.

The following Psalm 145, Lauda anima mea, is not said on the day of death, nor on the day of burial of the deceased, nor is it said on whatsoever day the Office is recited according to the rank of Double.

Psalm 145. Lauda, anima mea

Praise the Lord, O my soul: while I live, will I praise the Lord; * yea, as long as I have any being, I will sing praises unto my God.

2 O put not your trust in princes, * nor in the children of men, in whom is no salvation.

3 His spirit shall go forth, and he shall turn again to his earth, * in that day shall perish all their thoughts.

4 Blessed is he that hath the God of Jacob for his help, and whose hope is in the Lord his God: * who hath made heaven and earth, the sea, and all that therein is.

5 Who keepeth truth for ever, who executeth judgment unto them that suffer wrong; * who feedeth the hungry.

6 The Lord looseth them that are in fetters; * the Lord giveth light to the blind.

7 The Lord lifteth up them that are cast down; * the Lord loveth the righteous.

8 The Lord keepeth the strangers; he shall defend the fatherless and widow: * and destroy the ways of the ungodly.

9 The Lord shall reign for evermore, thy God, O Sion, * throughout all generations.

10 Eternal rest * grant unto them, O Lord.

11 And let perpetual light * shine upon them.

V. From the gates of hell.

R. Deliver his (her, their) soul(s), O Lord.

V. May he (she, they) rest in peace.

R. Amen.

V. O Lord, hear my prayer.

R. And let my cry come unto thee.

V. The Lord be with you.

R. And with thy spirit.

Let us pray.

O God, who didst cause thy servants, for whom we pray, to enjoy the dignity of the priesthood, and some to be bishops, after the order of thine Apostles: grant unto them, we beseech thee, finally to rejoice in the company of those Saints in heaven whose ministry they did sometime share on earth.

O God, who desirest not the death of a sinner but rather that all mankind should be saved: we beseech thee mercifully to grant that the brethren, kinsfolk, and benefactors of our congregation, who have passed out of this world, may by the intercession of blessed Mary Ever-Virgin and of all thy Saints come to enjoy with them everlasting blessedness.

O God, the Creator and Redeemer of all them that believe: grant unto the souls of thy servants and handmaidens the remission of all their sins; that as they have ever desired thy merciful pardon, so by the supplications of their brethren they may receive the same. Who livest and reignest with the Father, in the unity of the Holy Ghost, ever one God, world without end.

R. Amen.
V. Eternal rest grant unto them, O Lord.
R. And let perpetual light shine upon them.
V. May they rest in peace.
R. Amen.

Special Prayers For the Dead

Note these are said in place of the common prayer in Lauds and Vespers above.

Said on the day of burial only if the body be absent
Collect   Let us pray.

Absolve, O Lord, we pray thee, the soul(s) of thy servant(s) N. from every bond of sin, that though they (he, she) may be dead unto the world, yet they (he, she) may live unto thee: and that whatsoever sins they (he, she) may have committed through the frailty of the flesh in their (his, her) earthly conversation may be done away by the pardon of thy most merciful loving-kindness. Through Jesus Christ, thy Son our Lord. Who liveth and reigneth with thee, in the unity of the Holy Ghost, ever one God, world without end.

R. Amen.
Said on the day of burial only if the body be present
Collect   Let us pray.

O God, whose nature and property is ever to have mercy and to forgive, receive our humble petitions for the soul(s) of thy servant(s) (or handmaid(s) N., which thou hast commanded to depart out of this world: deliver them (him, her) not into the hand of the enemy, neither forsake them (him, her) at the last; but command them (him, her) to be received by the holy Angels, and brought to the country of paradise; that forasmuch as they (he, she) hoped and believed in thee, they (he, she) may not undergo the pains of hell, but be made partaker(s) of everlasting felicity. Through Jesus Christ, thy Son our Lord. Who liveth and reigneth with thee, in the unity of the Holy Ghost, ever one God, world without end.

R. Amen.

On the third, seventh, and thirtieth day after the burial of the deceased

Collect   Let us pray.

We beseech thee, O Lord, that the soul of thy servant N., whom three (or seven or thirty) days since we did commit unto the ground: may be made partaker of the fellowship of thine elect; and that thou wouldest pour upon him (her) the continual dew of thy mercy. Through Jesus Christ, thy Son our Lord. Who liveth and reigneth with thee, in the unity of the Holy Ghost, ever one God, world without end.

At the Year's-Mind

Collect   Let us pray.

O God, to whom alone belongeth the forgiveness of sins: grant, we pray thee, to the soul of thy servant(s) (or handmaid(s)), whose Year's-Mind we now keep, a place of rest and refreshment, peace and blessing, light and glory. Through Jesus Christ, thy Son our Lord. Who liveth and reigneth with thee, in the unity of the Holy Ghost, ever one God, world without end.

For a Sovereign Pontiff Departed

Collect   Let us pray.

O God, who of thy unspeakable providence didst vouchsafe to call thy servant N. to the number of thy high priests: grant, we beseech thee, that like as he did fulfil on earth the office of thine only-begotten Son, so he may evermore be numbered in the fellowship of them that therein have served thee faithfully. Through the same Jesus Christ, thy Son our Lord. Who liveth and reigneth with thee, in the unity of the Holy Ghost, ever one God, world without end.

For a Bishop Departed

Collect Let us pray.

O God, who in the ranks of the Apostolic Priesthood didst cause thy servant N. (thy servants N. and N.) to stand before thee in the high place of Bishop: grant, we beseech thee, that he (they) may be joined unto the company of such in everlasting blessedness. Through Jesus Christ, thy Son our Lord. Who liveth and reigneth with thee, in the unity of the Holy Ghost, ever one God, world without end.

For a Cardinal Bishop Departed

Collect Let us pray.

O God, who in the ranks of the Apostolic Priesthood didst cause thy servant N. (thy servants N. and N.) to stand before thee in the high place of Cardinal Bishop: grant, we beseech thee, that he (they) may be joined unto the company of such in everlasting blessedness. Through Jesus Christ, thy Son our Lord. Who liveth and reigneth with thee, in the unity of the Holy Ghost, ever one God, world without end.

For a Cardinal Priest Departed who had been consecrated Bishop

Collect Let us pray.

O God, who in the ranks of the Apostolic Priesthood didst cause thy servant N. (thy servants N. and N.) to stand before thee in the high place of Cardinal Priest: grant, we beseech thee, that he (they) may be joined unto the company of such in everlasting blessedness. Through Jesus Christ, thy Son our Lord. Who liveth and reigneth with thee, in the unity of the Holy Ghost, ever one God, world without end.

For a Cardinal Priest Departed who had not been consecrated Bishop

Collect Let us pray.

O God, who in the ranks of the Apostolic Priesthood didst cause thy servant N. (thy servants N. and N.) to stand before thee in the high place of Cardinal Priest: grant, we beseech thee, that he (they) may be joined unto the company of such in everlasting blessedness. Through Jesus Christ, thy Son our Lord. Who liveth and reigneth with thee, in the unity of the Holy Ghost, ever one God, world without end.

 For a Cardinal Deacon Departed who had been ordained Priest
 Collect Let us pray.

O God, who in the ranks of the Apostolic Priesthood didst cause thy servant N. (thy servants N. and N.) to stand before thee in the high place of Cardinal Deacon: grant, we beseech thee, that he (they) may be joined unto the company of such in everlasting blessedness. Through Jesus Christ, thy Son our Lord. Who liveth and reigneth with thee, in the unity of the Holy Ghost, ever one God, world without end.

 For a Cardinal Deacon Departed who had not been ordained Priest
 Collect Let us pray.

Incline thine ear, O Lord, unto the prayers whereby we humbly call upon thee to shew mercy unto the soul of thy servant and Cardinal Deacon N. which it hath pleased thee to call out of this world, that it may please thee also to set him in the abode of peace and light, and make partaker of the fellowship of thine elect. Through Jesus Christ, thy Son our Lord. Who liveth and reigneth with thee, in the unity of the Holy Ghost, ever one God, world without end.

 For a Priest Departed
 Collect Let us pray.

O God, who in the ranks of the Apostolic Priesthood didst cause thy servant N. (thy servants N. and N.) to stand before thee in the high place of Priest: grant, we beseech thee, that he (they) may be joined unto the company of such in everlasting blessedness. Through Jesus Christ, thy Son our Lord. Who liveth and reigneth with thee, in the unity of the Holy Ghost, ever one God, world without end.

 Another Collect for a Priest Departed
 Collect Let us pray.

Grant, we beseech thee, Almighty God, that the soul of thy servant N., whom, whilst he lived in this world, thou didst adorn with the holy office of thy Priesthood, may evermore rejoice in the glory of heavenly felicity. Through Jesus Christ, thy Son our Lord. Who liveth and reigneth with thee, in the unity of the Holy Ghost, ever one God, world without end.

For a Man Departed

Collect   Let us pray.

Incline thine ear, O Lord, unto the prayers whereby we humbly call upon thee to shew mercy unto the soul of thy servant N. which it hath pleased thee to call out of this world, that it may please thee also to set him in the abode of peace and light, and make partaker of the fellowship of thine elect. Through Jesus Christ, thy Son our Lord. Who liveth and reigneth with thee, in the unity of the Holy Ghost, ever one God, world without end.

For a Woman Departed

Collect   Let us pray.

We beseech thee, O Lord, of thy loving-kindness, to have mercy upon the soul of this thy handmaid N.: that, being purged from all the defilements whereby in this dying body she hath been defouled, she may be restored to her inheritance in everlasting salvation. Through Jesus Christ, thy Son our Lord. Who liveth and reigneth with thee, in the unity of the Holy Ghost, ever one God, world without end.

For Dead Brethren, Kinsfolk, and Benefactors

Collect   Let us pray.

O God, who desirest not the death of a sinner but rather that all mankind should be saved: we beseech thee mercifully to grant that the brethren, kinsfolk, and benefactors of our congregation, who have passed out of this world, may by the intercession of blessed Mary Ever-Virgin and of all thy Saints come to enjoy with them everlasting blessedness. Through Jesus Christ, thy Son our Lord. Who liveth and reigneth with thee, in the unity of the Holy Ghost, ever one God, world without end.

For a Father and Mother

Collect   Let us pray.

O God, who didst command thy people saying: Honour thy father and thy mother: of thy loving-kindness have mercy on the soul(s) of my father (and my mother) and forgive them (him, her) all their (his, her) sins; and I humbly pray thee that thou wouldest grant unto me to behold their faces (his, her face) in the glory of eternal felicity. Through Jesus Christ, thy Son our Lord. Who liveth and reigneth with thee, in the unity of the Holy Ghost, ever one God, world without end.

    For several Fathers and Mothers
    Collect   Let us pray.

O God, who didst command thy people saying: Honour thy father and thy mother: of thy loving-kindness have mercy on the souls of our parents and forgive them all their sins; and we humbly pray thee that thou wouldest grant unto us to behold their faces in the glory of eternal felicity. Through Jesus Christ, thy Son our Lord. Who liveth and reigneth with thee, in the unity of the Holy Ghost, ever one God, world without end.

Daily Pilgrimage to Purgatory

Origin Of The Daily Pilgrimage To Purgatory

In the writings of St. Margaret Mary we find the following exhortation: "In union with the divine Heart of Jesus make a short pilgrimage to Purgatory at night. Offer Him all your activities of the day and ask Him to apply His merits to the suffering souls. At the same time implore them to obtain for you the grace to live and die in the love and friendship of this divine Heart. May He never find in you any resistance to His holy will, nor any wish to thwart His designs in your regard. Fortunate will you be, if you succeed in obtaining deliverance for some of these imprisoned souls, for you will gain as many friends in heaven." This pious practice which St. Margaret Mary recommended to her novices for the octave of All Souls, was introduced to the members of the Arch-confraternity of Our Lady of the Sacred Heart in the year 1885. Since then many of the faithful have made this pilgrimage daily. Our world-wide Arch-confraternity, therefore, would seem to have been chosen by divine Providence to obtain comfort and deliverance for many souls in Purgatory. In a letter of recommendation, given on January 5, 1884, his Eminence, Cardinal Monaco la Valette, Vicar General of His Holiness, sanctioned the propagation of the "Daily Pilgrimage to Purgatory". On October 8 of the following year, his successor, Cardinal Parochi deigned not only to honour us with a letter of approbation, but also delivered a splendid sermon on this practice in the church of Our Lady of the Sacred Heart in Rome, in which it had been introduced. May it please the divine Heart of Jesus to use this booklet as a means of spreading this work of sympathetic love for the Poor Souls everywhere. May this most benevolent of hearts extend to all who in any way assist in its circulation, the fullness of His graces and blessings.

Advantages Of This Practice

It is short ...... A "Daily Pilgrimage" ...... It is requires little more of your time than an ordinary prayer, a religious thought, or a devout ejaculation.

It is easy …… It can be practised by any one without effort, regardless of age or state of life, at any time, and in any place.

It is comforting …… No more is required than to descend in spirit for a few moments into Purgatory; to petition God to send light, relief and peace to the holy souls: to relieve them of their sufferings, and to hasten the hour of their deliverance.

It is holy …… It is in accordance with the wishes of the Sacred Heart; it increases His honour. He is our companion on this pilgrimage. We share in his love, and receive from Him light, relief and peace for the suffering souls.

It is generous ……. It offers to the Sacred Heart every meritorious deed performed in the course of a day; prayers, mortifications, good works, alms, suffrages of every kind, and places them at His disposal on behalf of the Poor Souls.

It is inexhaustible …… It implores Our Lord and Saviour to apply to them the infinite merits of His Life, His Passion and Death, and also those of the Blessed Virgin Mary, St. Joseph and all The Saints. It is efficacious….. If only you knew with what ardent desire these holy souls long for this new "remedy" which has such efficacy to relieve their sufferings. For this is what St Margaret Mary calls the devotion to the Sacred Heart.

It is meritorious … By extending this act of brotherly love to the Poor Souls, our own merits are increased in the same measure as the pious thoughts which it inspired, the good disposition which it creates, the acts of virtue which it prompts. It goes on increasingly …… At every moment of the day and night, somewhere on earth members of the Archconfraternity pray for our departed friends according to our intention. There is an uninterrupted sequence of holy Masses, Stations of the Cross, good works, prayers and indulgences. Those whose death we mourn will never be forgotten. It is approved by the Church …… Many bishops have readily given their approval. His Eminence, the Cardinal Vicar of his Holiness, has recommended it twice in a most explicit manner. The Holy Father himself has deigned to bestow the richest privileges upon the altar of the Poor Souls in the Church of Our Lady of the Sacred Heart in Rome. It is favoured by God himself …… Numerous spiritual and temporal favours have manifested, again and again, how pleasing this practice is to the Sacred Heart. One may use it with confidence as a means of obtaining the conversion of a sinner, the restoration of health, or a special grace. Very effective also is the promise to promote this devotion if a petition be heard. If the Lord rewards in this life the gift of a cup of cold water, given in His name to the poor, He certainly will reward, even more generously, the help offered for His sake to the Poor Souls. It is salutary …… By helping the Poor Souls, we assure ourselves their perpetual gratitude; they will pray for us, especially after their entrance into eternal happiness; in particular will they endeavour to obtain for us the grace of a happy death. "On awakening on this morning on the Sunday of the Good Shepherd." wrote St. Margaret Mary two hundred fifty years ago, "two of my suffering friends came to take leave of me, today the Good Shepherd received them into His eternal home. They left with untold joy and happiness. When I asked them to remember me, they replied: "Ingratitude has never entered heaven." It deserves to be propagated …… O you my Christian friends who read these lines, priests, religious or devout lay-people, help to spread this devotion, It is so simple, and requires so little effort; moreover, you will be rewarded for it. Let at least one tiny drop of water trickle into Purgatory every day. If no one refuses to do so, many souls will be released, and a refreshing stream of grace will flow without ceasing through that prison of fire.

The Daily Pilgrimage To Purgatory
A Pious Union of Prayer

Its Object

"In union with the Divine Heart of Jesus make a short pilgrimage to Purgatory at night. Offer Him all your activities of the day and ask Him to apply His merits to the suffering souls. At the same time implore them to obtain for you the grace to live and die in the love and friendship of this divine Heart. May He never find in you any resistance to His holy will nor any wish to thwart His design in your regard. Fortunate will you be, if you succeed in obtaining deliverance for some of these imprisoned souls, for you will gain as many friends in heaven."

Its Purpose

The purpose of this "Pious Union" is to obtain relief and deliverance from Purgatory for the Poor Souls. Its secondary aim is the attainment of personal holiness, the conversion of sinners and the acquisition of the necessary spiritual and temporal graces. Its Privileges a. Special protection of the Sacred Heart, Who considers every act of charity towards the Poor Souls as done to Himself. b. Gratitude of the souls in Purgatory. "If only you knew," writes St. Margaret Mary, "with what great longing these holy souls yearn for this new remedy, which relieves them so effectively of their sufferings." For this is what they call true devotion to the Sacred heart, especially the sacrifice of the holy Mass offered in His honour." In another place the Saint says: "Ingratitude has never entered heaven." c. A share in the prayers and good works of the associates. d. The departed members of this "Pious Union," particularly those who have been specially recommended, receive unceasingly the fruits of the numerous holy Masses, offered for the intention of this association.

Its Obligations

a. Promise without binding yourself in conscience, to meditate every day, no matter how briefly, on Purgatory or some other pious practice, e.g. on some ejaculatory prayer to which indulgences applicable to the Poor Souls are attached. b. Send, if possible once a year, a holy Mass for the intention of this "Pious Union". Offer for the same intention all the Masses you attend, all the Holy Communions you receive, all the good works you perform, particularly those which have for their purpose the veneration of the Sacred Heart.

Remarks

Help to spread the devotion to the Sacred Heart, so dear and beneficial to the suffering souls. Distribute the booklet: "Daily

Pilgrimage to Purgatory." Enrol, if you have not yet done so, in the Archconfraternity of Our Lady of the Sacred Heart. All of its indulgences are applicable to the Poor Souls.

Indulgenced Prayers

Eternal Father, I offer Thee the Precious Blood of Jesus Christ in satisfaction for my sins, and in supplication for the Holy Souls in Purgatory, and for the needs of the Holy Church. (500 days. Plenary Indulgence once a month if said daily.)

Sweet Heart of Mary, be my salvation! (300 days. Plenary Indulgence once a month if said daily.)

My Jesus mercy! (300 days. Plenary Indulgence once a month if said daily)

Jesus, meek and humble of Heart, make my heart like unto Thine! (500 days, once a day. Plenary indulgence once a month if said daily)

May the Sacred Heart of Jesus be loved everywhere! (300 days.)

Our Lady of the Sacred Heart, pray for us! (300 days.)

St. Joseph, Model and Patron of those who love the Sacred Heart, pray for us! (300 days. Plenary Indulgence once a month.)

Prayers for the Daily Pilgrimage to Purgatory

Preparation: (Either one of the following acts or a similar one will suffice.)

Prayer - O St. Margaret Mary, whom the Lord has chosen to reveal to the whole world all the treasures hidden in his merciful heart of Love! O thou who hast heard how the Poor Souls in Purgatory begged for this new remedy, the devotion to the Sacred Heart which relieves them so effectively of their torments! O thou who hast set free so many of these poor prisoners by practising this devotion: obtain for us the grace to make this Pilgrimage worthily in the company of the Sacred Heart of Jesus. Amen. (Unite your own intentions with those of the faithful who make this pilgrimage daily.)

Consecration of the Day: Divine Heart of Jesus, in making this pilgrimage with Thee as my Companion, I consecrate to Thee all my thoughts, words and actions of the entire day. I pray Thee to unite my small merits with Thine and to apply them to the Poor Souls, especially the soul of Thy servant, N.N. Likewise do I entreat you, holy souls, to help me obtain the grace to persevere in love and loyalty toward the Sacred Heart, by submitting readily and without complaint to whatever designs He may have in my regard.

Offering - Eternal Father, we offer Thee the Blood, Passion and Death of Jesus Christ and the sorrows of the most holy Mary and St. Joseph in payment for our sins, in suffrage for the holy souls in Purgatory, for the wants of our Holy Mother the Church and for the conversion of Sinners. Amen.

Ejaculation - "May the Sacred Heart of Jesus be loved everywhere." (300 days)

"Our Lady of the Sacred Heart, pray for us." 300 days

"St. Joseph, model and patron of those who love the Sacred Heart, pray for us." (300 Days, Plenary Indulgence, once a month)

Preparatory Meditation: Let us for a moment, in company with the Sacred Heart, descend in spirit into the consuming flames of Purgatory. How many of these souls are beginning their painful imprisonment this very moment! I know many of them have been there for a long time and shall be there for a longer time to come! And what a holy legion almost entirely purified and cleansed at the present moment, shall rise to heaven this very day! How happy the

Poor Souls are! They have escaped hell forever. They are certain to obtain eternal happiness. They are friends of God; they are saved. And yet, how miserable they are at the same time. They must still suffer temporal punishment for sins which have been already forgiven them. The gates of their heavenly fatherland are still closed to them; they are sentenced to expiating fire. Behold them in their present plight! Listen to their lamentations! Speak to them a word of friendship and sympathy, and hasten to their assistance!

Sunday

Holy Souls in Purgatory, is there anything you regret when you think of your life on earth? I deeply regret wasted time... I did not consider it so precious, so fleeting, so irretrievable. For this reason my life was worth only half of what it might have been. Oh, had I but realized it then! Would that I could return to earth, how differently I would use the time given me! Precious time! ...... Today I know how to appreciate you. You were purchased with the blood of Christ: you were given me for the sole purpose of loving God, sanctifying myself and edifying my neighbour. But alas! I have abused you by committing sin; I have craved vanity, pleasures and trifles; I have been dreaming dreams which now cause me bitter reproaches and remorse. Precious time ...... Wasted time..... How heavily you weigh upon me now! How it grieves me to have lost you through my own fault! Fleeting time which passes so quickly on earth, but which drags so slowly in this prison of fire, in this place of excruciating torments! Formerly, years seemed like days to me. My whole life vanished like a dream. Hours now seem like years, days like centuries. I must now suffer, weep, and wait, until the last minute of wasted time is redeemed. Oh, how long shall my exile last! Irretrievable time! On earth I relied on my last years to do penance; but the thread of my life was severed at a moment when I expected it least! O precious time! You were given me to acquire treasures and graces without number, but now you are lost for me forever. You, who still live on earth, do not waste the gift of time, which has cost Jesus such a high price, and for which you too will have to suffer in Purgatory if you imitate our carelessness. You, who are privileged to live during a time which is pre-eminently devoted to the Sacred

Heart, during these last centuries when He has revealed to the world His love in its fullness: intercede for us that we may obtain the merits of at least one of these days, in which His grace is so freely and abundantly offered you.

Pious Exercises

Resolution - Today I will do everything possible to assist the souls of priests, religious and all those in Purgatory who have been faithful to this devotion all their lives. I also recommend myself to those who are entering heaven at this moment.

Thought for the day - The sufferings of the souls in Purgatory are so great that a single day appears to them like a thousand years.

Exercise - Use a few moments of your time to make ejaculations in honour of the divine Heart for the comfort and consolation of the Poor Souls.

Special Intention - Implore the divine Heart of Jesus to grant relief to the most forsaken soul in Purgatory.

Motive - The greater the abandonment of a soul, the greater will be its gratitude towards you. It will obtain for you the privilege never to be forsaken by God through the withdrawal of His grace, and never to abandon Him by committing sin.

Prayer - O Lord God Almighty, I pray Thee, by the Precious Blood which Thy divine Son Jesus shed in the garden, deliver the souls in Purgatory and especially that soul which is most destitute of spiritual aid; and vouchsafe to bring it to Thy glory, there to praise and bless Thee forever. Amen Our Father ......Hail Mary (The Faithful who devoutly offer prayers for the Poor Souls, with the intention of doing so for 7 or 9 successive days, may obtain: An indulgence of three years once each day; A plenary indulgence on the usual condition at the end of their 7 or 9 days of prayer. Any form of prayer for the Poor Souls may be used.)

De Profundis Psalm 129: Out of the depths I have cried unto Thee, O Lord: Lord hear my voice. Let Thine ears be attentive to the voice of my supplication. If Thou, O Lord, shalt mark our iniquities: O Lord, who can abide it? For with Thee there is mercy; and by reason of Thy law I have waited on Thee, O Lord. My soul hath waited on His word; my soul hath hoped in the Lord. From the morning watch even unto night: let Israel hope in the Lord. For with the Lord there is mercy; and with Him is plentiful redemption. And he shall redeem Israel from all his iniquities. V. Eternal rest grant unto them, O Lord. R. And let perpetual light shine upon them. (3 years; 5 years every day in November; Plenary indulgence once a month.)

Ejaculation:- Sweet Heart of Jesus, make me love Thee ever more and more. (300 days. Plenary indulgence once a month.)

Monday

Holy Souls in Purgatory, is there anything you regret when you think of your life on earth? I deeply regret my extravagance in the use of earthly possessions. . . My fortune, my health, my talent, my position in the world, the influence I had, my relatives, my servants, in a word, everything could have been of spiritual benefit to me if only I had known how to use it for the greater honour of the divine Heart. How many graces could I have drawn upon myself! This I neglected to do, and at the hour of my death, all my possessions have come to naught. Oh, were I but rich today in these my former possession! Would that I could use them to hasten even for one moment, the hour of my deliverance; to increase, even by one degree, the glory which God has in store for me; to awaken if only in one soul now living in the world, the devotion to the divine Heart of Jesus. My friends, whose fortunes are still at your disposal, use them for the support of your neighbour by generously giving alms to the poor. Use them for the greater honour of God as pious offerings designated for the propagation of the devotion to His Sacred Heart throughout the world.

Pious Exercises

Resolution. - Today I will do everything possible to assist the souls of the faithful departed from all parts of Europe. I also recommend myself to those who are entering heaven at this moment.

Thought for the day-- "The gates of heaven are opened by alms." (St. John Chrys. hom 32 in Ep. ad Heb.)

Exercise - Give an alms for the propagation of the devotion to the divine Heart of Jesus.

Special Intention - Pray for the soul which is nearest to heaven.

Motive - The closer a soul is to the end of its sufferings, the more ardently will it long for union with the Sacred Heart. Remove. therefore, by your prayers, the obstacles still in its way. In return, it will obtain for you the grace to sever the ties which now prevent you from giving yourself entirely to God.

Prayer - O Lord God Almighty. I pray Thee, by the Precious Blood which Thy divine Son Jesus shed in His cruel scourging, deliver the souls in Purgatory, and that soul especially which is nearest to its entrance into Thy glory; that so it may forthwith begin to praise and bless Thee forever. Amen. Our Father... Hail Mary.

Ejaculation.- Sweet Heart of Mary, be my salvation! (300 days. Plenary indulgence once a month.)

Tuesday

Holy Souls in Purgatory, is there anything you regret when you think of your life on earth? I deeply regret my neglect of so many splendid graces They have been offered to me in such abundance at every moment of my life and with such loving admonitions. Spiritual regeneration, vocation and sacraments; word of God, holy inspirations and good examples; graces to protect me in danger, to help me in temptations; the grace of forgiveness for my sins, of indulgences so easily gained ...... What an incalculable number of the most varied graces! Some of them I have refused: others I have accepted with coldness; unfortunately, I have misused most of them. I have preferred earthly possessions to the eternal. How I have deceived myself! Oh, could I but for one moment quench my thirst at the fountains of mercy, flowing from the Sacred Heart! Unfortunately these fountains are spurned by sinners as they were by me. You, who behold the inexhaustible stream of graces flow by, why do you not draw from it a few drops for yourself! Consider what St Margaret Mary says: "It is certain that everyone on earth could obtain salutary graces without number, if he but had a grateful love for Jesus Christ, such as is manifested by those who love and venerate His Sacred Heart."

Pious Exercises

Resolution -Today I will do everything possible to assist the souls of the faithful departed from all parts of Asia, particularly from Palestine and from countries infested with idolatry, schism and heresy. I also recommend myself to those who are entering heaven at this moment.

Thought for the day - "The benefit of a single grace is greater than all the material value of the whole world." (St Thomas I-II, Q113, A9 Ad2)

Exercise – In order to relieve the Poor Souls of their sufferings, I shall offer them today, by way of suffrage, the benefit of some indulgence gained by prayers or some devotional exercise in honour of the divine Heart of Jesus.

Special Intention - - Pray for the soul in Purgatory which is farthest from eternal rest.

Motive - . Let yourself be moved by the abandonment, resignation and humility with which that soul bears its long suffering: it will be grateful to you. Happy will you be, if it obtains for you the virtue of humility in this world, so that you may be exalted in the next.

Prayer.- O Lord Almighty, I pray Thee by the Precious Blood which Thy divine Son Jesus shed in the bitter crowning of thorns, deliver the souls in Purgatory, and in particular that soul which would be the last to depart out of this place of suffering, that it may not tarry so long before it comes to praise Thee in thy glory and bless Thee for ever. Amen. Our Father... Hail Mary.

Ejaculation - Eternal Father, I offer Thee the Precious Blood of Jesus Christ in satisfaction for my sins, and in supplication for the Holy Souls in Purgatory, and for the needs of the Holy Church. (500 days. Plenary indulgence once a month if said daily.)

Wednesday

Holy Souls in Purgatory, is there anything you regret when you think of your life on earth? I deeply regret the evil which I have done. In the world, evil seemed so easy, so pleasant. In the midst of pleasures I silenced the voice of conscience. Today my faults weigh me down; their bitterness torments me; their memory persecutes and tortures me. Mortal sins, forgiven, but not atoned for, venial sins, small imperfections. Too late to detest you in Purgatory! Just punishment must now take its course. Oh. if I could return to life again! No promise, be it ever so tempting, no riches, no flattery could induce me to commit even the smallest sin! My friends, you who are still free to choose between God and the world, gaze upon the crown of thorns. upon the cross, upon all the sufferings which your sins have brought upon the Sacred Heart! Think of the sorrow which these sins and faults will cause you in Purgatory, and you will be able to avoid them without effort. If you long for the grace to resist Satan when he tempts you, consider what St. Margaret Mary says: "I cannot believe that persons consecrated to this divine Heart will ever be lost; neither do I believe that they will fall into the hands of Satan by committing a mortal sin, after having given themselves entirely to Him. For they will make every effort to honour, love and glorify this divine Heart, and to follow his designs in their regard willingly and without reserve."

Pious Exercises

Resolution- Today I will do everything possible to assist the souls of the faithful departed from Africa, particularly from those countries in Africa which were formerly Catholic. I also recommend myself to those who are entering heaven at this moment.

Thought for the day - "What doth it profit a man, if he gain the whole world and suffer the loss of his own soul?" (Math. 16,25.)

Exercise- Make an act of contrition in union with the souls in Purgatory, before a picture of the Sacred Heart.

Special intention - Pray for the soul richest in merits.

Motive - The more exalted a soul is in heaven, the more effective will be its request for true love of God for you, without which there is no real merit.

Prayer - O Lord God Almighty, I pray Thee, by the Precious Blood which Thy divine Son Jesus shed in the streets of Jerusalem, when He carried the Cross upon His sacred shoulders, deliver the souls in Purgatory, and especially that soul which is richest in merits before Thee, that so. in that throne of glory which awaits it, it may magnify Thee and bless Thee forever. Amen. Our Father... Hail Mary.

Ejaculation -- Jesus, Mary, Joseph. I give you my heart and my soul. Jesus, Mary, Joseph, assist me in my last agony. Jesus, Mary, Joseph, may I breathe forth my soul in peace with you. (Seven years for each invocation. Plenary indulgence once a month.)

Thursday

Holy Souls in Purgatory, is there anything you regret when you think of your life on earth? I deeply regret the scandal which I have given! Oh, if I had to grieve over my own faults only ... If only I would have prevented, in the hour of my health, the disastrous consequences of the scandal of which I was the cause. If only I could detain from this place of darkness the many souls that followed my sad example and listened to my pernicious teachings! But no! Through my fault the evil goes on, and perhaps, will spread over a period of years and centuries. And now I have to give an account of all the sins for which I am to blame!

Oh, were I but able to let my sad words resound unto the ends of the earth and to wander through the world as a preacher of penance! With what untiring zeal would I labour among souls in order to estrange them from evil and return them to virtue. Oh you my friends on earth, who come to visit me in this dark prison in order to let a ray of salutary light shine upon me: you shall find in the Sacred Heart the surest and easiest way of bringing back to God as many souls as I have led into sin by bad example! Tell them that "this divine Heart is a fortress and a sanctuary for those who desire to escape divine justice by seeking refuge in Him. For the number of sins committed at the present time is so great, that they challenge a just Creator to punish the sinner swiftly and severely."

Resolution - Today I will do everything possible to assist the souls of the faithful departed from North and South America, especially those from my native town. I also recommend myself to those who are entering heaven at this moment.

Thought for the day - "The Son of man will render to everyone according to his works." (Math. 16.27).

Exercise - Give to someone a picture or a book treating of the Sacred Heart.

Special Intention- Pray for the soul which had the greatest devotion to the Most Blessed Sacrament.

Motive - That soul will obtain for you the grace to receive Holy Communion worthily at the hour of death as a pledge of your eternal salvation.

Prayer- O Lord God Almighty, I pray Thee, by the Precious Blood of Thy divine Son Jesus, which He gave with His own hands upon the eve of His Passion to His beloved Apostles to be their food and drink, and which He left to His whole Church to be a perpetual sacrifice and live-giving food of His own faithful people, deliver the souls in Purgatory, and especially that one which was most devoted to this mystery of infinite love, that it may with Thy same divine Son, and with Thy Holy Ghost, ever praise Thee for Thy love therein in eternal glory. Amen. Our Father... Hail Mary.

Ejaculation - My Jesus! Mercy! (300 days. Plenary indulgence once a month.)

Friday

Holy Souls in Purgatory, is there anything you regret when you think of your life on earth? I deeply regret my neglect of acts of mortification. How easy they would have been on earth, but how difficult they are now in Purgatory. Here the smallest suffering is more poignant than the most cruel torments on earth. In the world it meant only patience and resignation in the hardships and adversities of my life; it meant only giving from my surplus to the poor, and devoting myself to works of atonement; it meant only gaining Indulgences and performing works of piety. Nothing could have been easier, and my Purgatory would have been shortened considerably. If God would but grant me the grace to exchange the years during which I must still remain in this place of sorrow for as many years of life on earth! No commands would be too severe for me; no pains could frighten me; the most difficult works of penance would be sweet and give me comfort at the thought of this consuming fire. You who now smart under the insignificant trials and hardships of this life! You who now earn your daily bread by the sweat of your brow, rejoice! The smallest suffering endured in the spirit of atonement and offered to the Sacred Heart in the spirit of expiation, will save you from a long and painful Purgatory.

Pious Exercises

Resolution - Today I will do everything possible to assist the souls of the faithful departed from the far distant countries of Oceania. I also recommend myself to those who are entering heaven at this moment.

Thought for the day- - "Bring forth therefore worthy fruits of penance." (Luke 3,8.)

Exercise - Offer to the Sacred Heart a little act of mortification for the relief of the suffering souls in Purgatory.

Special Intention -- Pray for the souls for which you are most bound to pray.

Motive - If you are indebted to these souls by an obligation of justice, do not postpone it, because this may call down the wrath of God upon yourself.

Prayer - O Lord God Almighty, I pray Thee, by the Precious Blood which Thy divine Son shed on this day upon the wood of the cross, especially from His most sacred hands and feet, deliver the souls in Purgatory, and in particular that soul for which I am most bound to pray; that no neglect of mine may hinder it from praising Thee in Thy glory and blessing Thee forever. Amen. Our Father. . . Hail Mary.

Ejaculation -- - Jesus, meek and humble of heart, make my heart like unto thine. (500 days. Plenary indulgence once a month.)

Saturday

Holy Souls in Purgatory, is there anything you regret when you think of your life on earth? I deeply regret the little amount of charity I have shown towards the Poor Souls during my life on earth. I could have been of such great service to them, since a Catholic can bring so much light and peace to these poor, suffering prisoners. I could have helped them by my prayers, mortifications, alms, good works, holy communions, spiritual communions and holy Masses, the latter, either by having them said for the Poor Souls or by attending them, especially those celebrated in honour of the Sacred Heart. I would have obtained numerous graces which would have made it easier for me to avoid sin. Moreover, I would have deserved a much shorter and less painful Purgatory, and now I would receive a much greater share in the prayers which were said for us wherever there are Catholics. Oh, could I but return to the world to help the Poor Souls! I certainly would interest myself in their sad plight! What devout prayers would I say for them! How solicitous I would be to awaken in the faithful the most tender sympathy and pity for them.

Pious Exercises

Resolution - Today I will do everything possible to assist the souls of the faithful departed from the missions fields of Melanesia and Micronesia. (New Ireland, New Britain, the Solomon, Gilbert and Marshall Islands and New Guinea.) I also recommend myself to those who are entering heaven at this moment.

Thought for the day - Thus spoke the guilt-burdened brothers of innocent Joseph one to another: "We deserve to suffer these things, because we have sinned against our brother, seeing the anguish of his soul, when he besought us, and we would not hear; therefore, is this affliction come upon us." (Gen. 42,21).

Exercise - Spread, as much as possible, the devotion "Daily Pilgrimage to Purgatory." The Poor Souls will be grateful to you.

Special Intention - Pray for the soul which had the greatest devotion to Our Lady of the Sacred Heart.

Motive - In doing so you cause the Mother of God great delight: she will obtain for you, through the intercession of this soul, the grace of a true devotion to the Sacred Heart.

Prayer - - O Lord God Almighty, I beseech Thee, by the Precious Blood, which gushed forth from the side of Thy Divine Son Jesus, in the sight of, and to the extreme pain of His most holy Mother, deliver the souls in Purgatory, and especially that soul which was the most devout to Our Lady of the Sacred Heart and Queen of Heaven; that it may soon attain unto Thy glory, there to praise Thee in her, and her in Thee, world without end. Amen. Our Father... Hail Mary.

Ejaculation - Our Lady of the Sacred Heart, pray for us! (300 days.)

Novena For The Relief Of The Poor Souls In Purgatory

by Fr. J. F. Durin, A Missionary Of The Sacred Heart
"He that stoppeth his ear against the cry of the poor, shall also cry himself and shall not be heard." (Prov. XXI, 13.)

To The Pious Reader

We present this small treatise to pious persons, entreating them to peruse it. Long ago the Holy Ghost said: "It is a holy and wholesome thing to pray for the dead, that they may be loosed from their sins." (II Macabees 12:46) Our Lord shed tears in seeing the tomb of Lazarus, and the Church, well acquainted with the feelings of her Divine Founder, is incessantly recommending charity for the Souls suffering in Purgatory. One of her eminent doctors, St. Thomas of Aquinas, has said that: "Of all prayers, the most meritorious, the most acceptable to God are prayers for the dead, because they imply all the works of charity, both corporal and spiritual."

But there are many people unconscious of the fact that charity for the "Poor Souls" is profitable to the living as well as to the dead. It is the teaching of the most learned theologians, viz: St. Alphonsus Ligori, Sylvius, Robert Bellarmine, Bonacina, and Suarez. "It is true," says St. Alphonsus, "they are unable to pray or merit anything for themselves, yet, when they pray for others, they are heard by God." Let us refer to Bellarmine: "The Souls in Purgatory," says he, "can pray for those, who address to them their petitions, and obtain from God help, forgiveness, assistance against temptations, and, all favors, both temporal and spiritual, which they may need."

Many Saints have experienced this wonderful assistance. St. Catherine of Bologna assured her Sisters that: "She obtained many favors by the prayers of the holy Souls in Purgatory, which she had asked in vain, through the intercession of the Saints." St. Theresa affirms that: "She always obtained the favors which she asked from God, through the intercession of the Poor Souls." We read also in the book of St. Bridget's Revelations that: "Being one day conducted by an Angel into Purgatory, she heard a soul say: "Oh Lord, vouchsafe to reward those who assist us! Return hundredfold blessings to those who help us and introduce us into the light of Heaven." St. Leonard of Port Maurice emphatically affirms that: "The blessed Souls, delivered by our prayers, will come down from Heaven to assist us in our temporal and spiritual affairs." The Venerable Cure d' Ars, replying to a priest said: "If one knew what we may obtain from God by the intercession of the Poor Souls, they would not be so much abandoned. Let us pray a great deal for them, they will pray for us."

Blessed Margaret Mary Alacoque had a special devotion for the Souls in Purgatory and has often accepted the charge of suffering for them. "Would that you knew," she said, "how my soul was replenished with joy, when speaking to those Souls, and seeing them immersed in glory as in a deep ocean. As I requested them to pray for you, they replied: "An ungrateful soul is not to be found in Heaven!" No, we cannot be deceived! If we have an ardent charity, a sincere piety, a true devotedness for the Poor Souls, we will be favored with their protection.

Let us try it! When we are in trouble, when we long for a favor, let us perform some pious or charitable work for the relief of the "Poor Souls." They will be grateful, they will plead for us, and present our requests to the Eternal Father, Who loves them.

May God bless this humble work! May He deign to enkindle generous hearts with zeal for the "Poor Souls."

"Blessed are the merciful: for they shall obtain mercy." (Matt., V., 7.)

Preparatory Prayer

(To be said every day of the novena.)

Act of Faith: My God, I believe in Thee, because Thou art Truth itself; I firmly believe the truths revealed to the Church.

Act of Hope: My God, I hope in Thee, because Thou art infinitely good.

Act of Charity: My God, I love Thee with all my heart, and above all things, because Thou are infinitely perfect; and I love my neighbor as myself, for the love of Thee.

De Profundis (Psalm 129)

(To be said every day of the novena.)

Out of the depths I have cried to Thee, O Lord: Lord hear my voice.

Let Thy ears be attentive to the voice of my supplication.

If Thou, O Lord, wilt mark iniquities; Lord, who shall stand it?

For with Thee there is merciful forgiveness: and by reason of Thy law,

I have waited for Thee, O Lord.

My soul hath relied on His word: my soul hath hoped in the Lord.

From the morning-watch even until night, let Israel hope in the Lord.

Because with the Lord there is mercy: and with Him plentiful redemption.

And He shall redeem Israel from all his iniquities.

V. Eternal rest give unto them. O Lord.

R. And let perpetual light shine upon them.

V. From the gate of Hell.

R. Deliver their souls, O Lord.

V. May they rest in peace.

R. Amen.

V. Lord, hear my prayer.

R. And let my cry come unto Thee.

V. The Lord be with you.

R. And with Thy Spirit.

Let us pray: O God, the Creator and Redeemer of all the faithful, we beseech Thee to grant to the Souls of Thy servants the remission of their sins, so that by our prayers they may obtain pardon for which they long. O Lord, Who livest and reignest, world without end. Amen.

May they rest in peace. Amen.

First Day: Existence of Purgatory

Say Preparatory Prayer

Meditation: There is a place for the purification of Souls which, after death, are yet stained with venial sins, or have not yet entirely satisfied for their pardoned sins. The Holy Catholic Church teaches it. I believe it firmly. By the light of the flames of Purgatory, I understand better Thy holiness, Thy Justice, Thy Mercy, O my God! "Who shall ascend into the mountain of the Lord? or who shall stand in His Holy Place? The innocent in hands, and clean of heart." (Ps. 23.) "There shall not enter into Heaven anything defiled." (Apoc. 21.) For Thou art Holy! Holy! Holy! O Lord, inspire my soul with the horror of sin! Grant me the grace to atone for my faults here below! Thou art just, O Lord, and Thy judgments are right. Who will dare to say: "Do not condemn me: tell me why Thou judgest me so?" (Job, X, 2.) "To Thee only have I sinned, and have done evil before Thee." (Ps. 50, 6.) I have deserved eternal punishment, but Thy mercy will follow me---it will follow me into the depth of death, and I will be spared.

Oh, Purgatory! where reigns Hope! There I will say with the Prophet: "When I was in distress Thou hast enlarged me!" (Ps. IV., 1.) If there were no Purgatory, where would so many lazy, negligent, unmortified souls go? "Blessed be the God and Father of our Lord Jesus Christ, the Father of mercies, and the God of all comfort, Who comforteth us in all our tribulation." (II Cor. 1., 3., 4.)

Practice: To pray the Divine Heart of Jesus that He deign to enkindle many souls with an ardent charity for the Souls in Purgatory.

Resolution: Every day of my life I will pray or do some good work for the "Poor Souls."

Example: It is related in the Acts of St. Perpetua, Martyr, that, being thrown into prison, she was favored with a vision. She saw her young brother, Dinocrates, in a dark place. He was surrounded by flames, thirsty, his face was ugly, pale, covered with an ulcer, which caused his death, when seven years old. She prayed fervently for him during seven days, and then he appeared to her in a very different condition. He was bright, clothed with a beautiful white dress, and there was no ulcer on his face. She understod that he had been delivered.

Prayer: De Profundis

Let us pray for our departed parents: O God, Who has commanded us to honor our Father and Mother, have pity on them, deliver them from the pains which they have deserved, and grant that I may see them in the glory of Heaven. Through our Lord Jesus Christ. Amen.

V. Eternal rest give unto them, O Lord.
R. And let perpetual light shine upon them.
V. May they rest in peace.
R. Amen.

Second Day: Pains of Purgatory

Say Preparatory Prayer

Meditation: Let us go with our Guardian Angel to Purgatory, to that place where the Divine Justice purifies Souls before they are admitted into Heaven.

There we will meet again our parents and our friends. Had this devotion no other advantage than that of reminding us of our departed ones, we should be grateful to God for such a consolation.

Oh, my father! Oh, my mother! Oh, brothers! Oh, sisters! Oh, friends! I had forgotten you! What do you suffer, beloved Souls? What shall I do to deliver you?

Our pains, they reply, are beyond description. When separated from our body, we saw the face of God, our Supreme Good, the Infinite Perfection. Then would we rush into His bosom, but we were driven back by His Justice, we were banished! Oh, no! on earth below you will never understand our pain, our grief, because we are separated from God! Your troubles, your sorrows, are the mere shadow of our affliction. But we suffer through our fault. If we would return to our former place on earth, we would be glad to accept the hardest mortification in exchange for Purgatory. "Have pity on me, have pity on me, at least you my friends, because the hand of the Lord hath touched me!" (Job. 19, 21.) Appease the Divine Justice with your good works, pay our debts, hasten the day when we shall enter into Heaven, and then we will return our gratitude forever.

Practice: Encourage all the works established for the relief of the Souls in Purgatory.

Resolution: At night, in the examination of conscience, I will question myself: What have you done today for the relief of Poor Souls?

Example: The soul of a pious lady, deceased at Luxemburg, appeared on All Saints' Day to a young girl of great piety, to beg the assistance of her prayers. When the latter was going to church, when approaching the holy rails, she was followed by the soul. Outside the church it could not be seen. As the young girl inquired the reason for it, she was answered: "You cannot understand how painful it is to be away from God. I am attracted to God by impetuous transports, by intolerable anxiety, and I am condemned to live far away from Him. My sorrow is so intense, that the ardor of fire, which surrounds me, is a lesser suffering. To soothe my pain, God, in His mercy, has allowed me to come into this church, and to adore Him, veiled under the Host, until I might see Him face to face in Heaven." She entreated the young girl to pray for her deliverance. It was done with so much fervor, that, on the 10th of December, the soul appeared, as bright as the sun, going to Heaven.

Prayer: De Profundis

Let us pray for our benefactors and friends: O God, Who bestowest forgiveness and salvation, we address Thy clemency that, through the intercession of the blessed Virgin Mary and of all the Saints, the Souls of our departed brethren, relatives and benefactors, may be admitted into the eternal glory. Through our Lord Jesus Christ. Amen.

V. Eternal rest give unto them, O Lord.
R. And let perpetual light shine upon them.
V. May they rest in peace.
R. Amen.

Third Day: The Pain of Loss

Say Preparatory Prayer

Meditation: During the long captivity, God's people, sitting on the shores of the Euphrates, moaned and cried in remembering Sion. So the Souls in Purgatory, plaintive and doleful, long for the joys of the heavenly mansion. They have had a glimpse of its glory and happiness, but because they were too much attached to earthly pleasures, they will be deprived, perhaps for a long time, of the celestial joys. They remember all the negligence of their former life, which now obstructs their way to Heaven. What sorrows! what remorses! because they have preferred a moment of pleasure to the enjoyment of Heaven. Then the poor, desolate Souls accuse themselves, saying with the Prophet: "I know my iniquity, and my sin is always before me." (Ps. 50, 5)

Since God has granted us the power of paying the debts of the "Poor Souls" with our works, let us appreciate this immense privilege. A noble heart should be delighted in relieving the poor, in consoling the afflicted, in bringing peace and happiness to those who suffer. Such is the privilege of those who assist the Souls suffering in Purgatory, because they deliver them from the hardest captivity and they open to them the gates of Heaven.

Moreover our charitable deeds for the "Poor Souls" will secure for us the gratitude of God Himself. "When," said our Lord to His holy servant Gertrude, "a Soul is liberated by your prayers, I accept it, as if I had been Myself liberated from captivity, and I will assuredly reward you according to the abundance of My mercy."

Practice: Perform today an act of mortification or obedience for the relief of the "Poor Souls."

Resolution: Be faithful in little things. Everything is great which is done for the Glory of God.

Example: At the close of September, 1870, there died at GH, France, a banker, renowned for his piety and his charity. By Divine permission his Soul appeared to his daughter, a member of a sisterhood in Belgium, to implore the assistance of her prayers. At first he was seen surrounded by flames, saying: "Have pity on your father, my child! If Purgatory were known, everyone would strive to escape its torments." Sometimes he would loudly complain: "I thirst! I thirst!"

Fervent prayers were offered for him at the convent, and he appeared again, enveloped in a dark cloud, but free from fire. He said to his daughter: "It seems that I am here during a century. My great suffering now is the thirst for the Vision of God and the enjoyment of His presence. I rush to Him and I am incessantly repulsed into the abyss because I have not yet paid all my debt to the Divine Justice."

Prayers were continued and on Christmas night he was seen in a halo of light, and addressing his daughter, said: "My pains are over. I owe this favor to the prayers offered for me. I come to thank you and your community. I will not forget you in Heaven."

Prayer: De Profundis

Let us pray for Bishops and Priests deceased: O God, Who has deigned to raise to the pontifical or sacerdotal dignity Thy servants N. N., grant us the grace of enjoying with them eternal felicity. Through our Lord Jesus Christ. Amen.

V. Eternal rest give unto them, O Lord.
R. And let perpetual light shine upon them.
V. May they rest in peace.
R. Amen.

Fourth Day: The Pain of Sense

Say Preparatory Prayer

Meditation: The pain of loss, the deprivation of the Vision of God, constitutes the supreme suffering in Purgatory. To this suffering of deprivation other sufferings of a positive nature are added. These are conditioned by the number and gravity of the sins which call for expiation and we have every reason to conceive of them as alike terrible and prolonged. Though the Church has not pronounced any decision on this point, it is the opinion of its doctors that the Souls in Purgatory are tormented by fire which penetrates them and burns them as gold in the crucible (Prov. 17, 3) until it has reduced them to such a degree of purity, that they may be worthy to appear before God.

When a fire is raging, everybody is excited. The people rush to the spot and everyone tries to save those who are already surrounded by the terrible element. Why are we unmoved at the sight of so many Souls who are tormented in the fire of Purgatory and who claim our assistance? Let us not abandon them.

Practice: Let us pray our Lord today to apply the merit of His death on the Cross to the Souls in Purgatory.

Resolution: I will observe the abstinence and fast prescribed by the Church, unless prevented by sickness.

Example: Two Spanish monks, bound together by a long and warm friendship, agreed that: if God would allow it, the one who should die first, would appear to the other to make known his condition in the other world. Some time later, one of them died, and appeared to his friend, saying: "I am saved, but condemned to suffer in Purgatory. It is impossible to describe such torments. Will you allow me to give you a sensible demonstration?" Then he placed his hand on the table and imprinted on it a mark as deep as if it had been made by a red hot iron. This table was preserved at Zamora (Spain) up to within the last century.

Prayer: De Profundis

Let us pray for a deceased man: Hear, O Lord, the prayers which we address to Thy mercy, and grant us that the soul of Thy servant N.N., which is gone into another world, be received into the abode of light and happiness to enjoy the felicity of the Saints. Through our Lord Jesus Christ. Amen.

V. Eternal rest give unto them, O Lord.
R. And let perpetual light shine upon them.
V. May they rest in peace.
R. Amen.

The Fifth Day: Duration of Purgatory

Say Preparatory Prayer

Meditation: How long do the pains last in Purgatory? Nobody knows. God has allowed some Souls to appear to their friends and benefactors to announce their departure for Heaven, but it seldom happened, and we cannot draw any conclusion from such cases. The period of confinement in Purgatory is probably much longer than we are inclined to think. Oh! how much combustible matter---how many imperfections, venial sins and temporal punishments due to mortal and venial sins---do you think they took with them to be cancelled in the flames of Purgatory? Centuries may pass until Divine Justice is satisfied and the Poor Soul is so purified as to be admitted to the Vision of God. The Venerable Bede relates that it was revealed to Drithelm, a great servant of God, that the Souls of those who spend their whole lives in the state of mortal sin, and are converted only on their death bed, are doomed to suffer the pains of Purgatory to the day of Last Judgment. Father Faber, commenting on this subject, says very justly: "We are not to leave off too soon praying for our parents, friends or relatives, imagining with a foolish and unenlightened esteem for the holiness of their lives, that they are freed from Purgatory much sooner than they really are!"

Let us consider the purity which is necessary to a soul, before being admitted into the presence of God! Let us remember the multitude of our venial sins, and see what light penance we have done for them. On the Day of Judgment the book of our deeds will be opened, and then we will be obliged to pay the last farthing. How guilty we are in abandoning so easily the Souls who need our assistance so much! The Saints are wiser. St. Monica, the mother of St. Augustine, was dead for twenty years, and she was still remembered by her son in the Holy Sacrifice. St. Ambrose promised solemnly and publicly to pray, during his entire life, for the soul of Theodosius the Great.

And supposing that we had delivered the Souls of our relatives and friends, have we emptied the prison of Purgatory?

How many poor, abandoned Souls linger in such horrible pains, imploring the assistance of some charitable heart. Cardinal Belllarmine has affirmed that: "Some Souls would suffer in Purgatory till the Day of Judgment, if they were not relieved by the prayer of the Church." Therefore, he authorizes the foundation of Masses to be said in perpetuity.

Practice: Would it not be a holy thought to form, among relatives and friends, an association of seven members, so that each would employ a day of the week for the relief of the "Poor Souls."

Resolution: Each time I hear the clock strike, I will say:

V. Eternal rest give unto them, O Lord.

R. And let perpetual light shine upon them.

(50 days each time for saying this V. and R., applicable only to the dead. Leo XIII Br., March 22, 1902.)

Example: Sister Denis, one of the first members of the order of the Visitation, was a zealous promoter of the devotion of the "Poor Souls." It was revealed to her that a prince, one of her relatives, had been condemned to suffer in Purgatory until the Day of Judgment. She offered herself as a victim for the relief of this soul. On her death-bed she said to the mother-superior that she had obtained for the poor soul the remittance of some hours of his pain. As the superior wondered at this fact, she replied: "O Mother, time in Purgatory is not counted as on earth; years passed here in sorrow, in poverty, in sickness, in suffering, are nothing, if we compare them with one hour in Purgatory!"

Prayer: De Profundis

Let us pray for a deceased woman: We humbly request Thee, O Lord, to grant mercy to the soul of Thy Servant, N. N., in order that, being delivered from the contagion of sin, she may enter into eternal salvation. Through our Lord Jesus Christ. Amen.

V. Eternal rest give unto them, O Lord.
R. And let perpetual light shine upon them.
V. May they rest in peace.
R. Amen.

The Sixth Day: Obligation of Assisting the "Poor Souls."

Say Preparatory Prayer

Meditation: The Souls in Purgatory cannot help themselves; they are unable to shorten their captivity. This reason alone should urge us to come to their assistance.

After death there is no more place for mercy, the time for justice commences. The soul is no longer free to choose between good and evil, therefore she cannot obtain any merit and her sufferings are accounted only as a payment for her debts. Alas! to be condemned to such sufferings, to be afflicted perhaps during centuries! How bad it is for those "Poor Souls!"

Could we see an unfortunate man, lying on the road, wounded, bleeding and would we pass and abandon him! We hold the key of a prison, crowded with prisoners; they crave for liberty and shall we leave them in their pitiable situation! So we have received from the mercy of God the privilege of liberating the Souls detained in Purgatory. We may say that we are the Providence of the dead; we, and we alone, may open the gates of Heaven to the Souls who are longing for their deliverance. It is the teaching of the Church, that the prayer of the living can be applied to the Souls in Purgatory. As your prayers ascend to Heaven, graces come down as a refreshing shower, bringing to the Souls forgiveness, liberty, and glory. The supplications of Mary and Martha obtained the resurrection of Lazarus. Let us address our prayers to the heart of Jesus, and we will deliver from their pains our dear departed ones. Shall we not be guilty if we do not employ our credit in favor of the unfortunate prisoners in Purgatory?

Practice: St. John Chrysostom recommended to every Christian family that they have a box at some convenient place in the house and that they put into it pennies, which will be used to have Masses said for the "Poor Souls."

Resolution: Pray today for the most abandoned Souls.

Example: At the Benedictine monasteries, when one of the monks died, his ordinary meals are distributed among the poor during thirty days. In the year 830, when a terrible plague was raging, many religious died. The abbot Rabanun Maurus gave the order to distribute the alms, according to the ancient usage, but the procurator did not obey. One night the stingy monk, having been delayed by his work, to shorten his way to his cell, passed through the Chapter room. There he was surrounded by all the monks, recently dead, who whipped him, leaving him half dead on the floor. Early the next morning he was found by the religious, who were going to the chapel. He related the event, made his confession, received the last rites and died two days afterwards.

Prayer: De Profundis

Let us pray: We humbly beseech Thee, O Lord, to release the Souls of Thy Servants, in order that they may obtain the glory of the resurrection and that they may be joined to the Saints and elect in Heaven. Through our Lord Jesus Christ. Amen.

V. Eternal rest give unto them, O Lord.
R. And let perpetual light shine upon them.
V. May they rest in peace.
R. Amen.

The Seventh Day: Cruelty of Those Who Abandon the "Poor Souls."

Say Preparatory Prayer

Meditation: Our Lord reproved the cruelty of the rich man, who refused even the crumbs of his table to poor Lazarus. while he himself was feasting sumptuously every day. Are they not imitating the wicked rich, who stand unmoved, seeing the sufferings of the "Poor Souls?" Those unfortunates, who appeal to our compassion, are not strangers. Among them there are our parents, our benefactors, our friends. Not long ago, they were living among us in the same house. We bear their names, we inherited their lands; and we forgot them! We abandon them! They may say with Job: "My kinsmen have forsaken me, and they that knew me have forgotten me. They that dwell in my house, and my maid-servants, have counted me as a stranger, and I have been like an alien in their eyes." (Job 19, 15) To forget the dead is a crime. Solemn promises were made at the death-bed. A child has said to his father and to his mother dying: I will not forget you! But where is the sign of this remembrance? Does it pray for them? Perhaps a vague, shadowy remembrance of the departed comes to its mind, but where is the profit to the "Poor Souls?" Useless and vain compassion! Empty love! Where are the works, alms, and holy Masses to assist, to relieve, to deliver the "Poor Souls?" Those who forget them will also be abandoned! "With what measure you mete, it shall be measured to you again." (St. Matt. 7, 22)

Practice: After the Evening Angelus say: Our Father and Hail Mary, once; or the De Profundis, as a daily tribute to the "Poor Souls."

Resolution: I will endeavor to propagate devotion to the "Poor Souls."

Example: A poor servant-girl had the pious custom of having a Mass said every month for the Souls in Purgatory, and she prayed especially for the Soul that was nearest to Heaven. After a long, protracted illness, she was leaving the hospital and setting out in search of a position. On her way she passed a church and, remembering that her monthly Mass had not been said, she entered the sacristy, requesting the priest to say this Mass. When she left the church a young man came up to her. He was tall and pale, and of a noble demeanor. "My good girl," he said, "I think you are looking for a position." "Yes," said the girl, somewhat surprised. "Well," said the young man, "if you go to Mrs. N. (here he named the street and number), I think you will find a good place;" and suddenly he disappeared among the crowd of passersby. The girl went, found the house, was introduced, and presented her petition. "But," said the lady of the house, "who could have sent you here? Nobody knows that I need a servant." Suddenly the girl, looking at the wall, noticed a portrait. "Look here, madam," said she, pointing to the picture, "that is the exact likeness of the man who told me to come here." At these words the old lady turned pale. "Ah!" said she, "that is the portrait of my son, who died two years ago. You shall henceforward remain with me, not as a servant-girl, but as my daughter, and we will always pray together for the "Poor Souls" in Purgatory."

Prayer: De Profundis

Let us pray: May our prayers be profitable, O Lord, to the Souls of Thy servants, that being absolved from their sins, they may have a share in the fruits of redemption. Through Our Lord Jesus Christ. Amen.

V. Eternal rest give unto them, O Lord.
R. And let perpetual light shine upon them.
V. May they rest in peace.
R. Amen.

The Eighth Day: The Communion of Saints

Say Preparatory Prayer

Meditation: How grand and consoling is the doctrine of the Communion of Saints! While we, in this world, are struggling for the celestial crown, and assist our brethren in Purgatory, we are protected by those who are triumphing in Heaven. We form, in reality, but one and the same family here below, in Purgatory, and in Heaven. If a member of our body is suffering, all other members come to its assistance. God loves the Souls in Purgatory as His dear spouses. He would open to them the gates of Heaven, but there are barriers. Let us present to His justice our prayers, our good works, and the obstruction will be removed; God will be satisfied.

It is often an obligation of justice to pray for the Poor Souls, but it is always a duty imposed by charity and by the compassion which we owe to one another.

There are in Purgatory Souls abandoned even by their parents and their friends, and for whom no one cares. Forgotten is their life, no thinking of it anymore; forgotten is their name; forgotten is their grave, which is visited no more; forgotten is their Soul, which is lingering in the fire of Purgatory. How their pain is increased by such neglect; They may say with the Prophet: "I am forgotten as one dead from the heart. I am become as a vessel that is destroyed." (Ps. 30, 30.)

Practice: Let us pray often and do some good works for the most abandoned Souls. Let us be to them like a father, a mother, a sister, a friend.

Resolution: To offer the abandonment of our Lord Jesus, in His passion, for the most abandoned Souls.

Example: Catherine of Cortona was hardly eight years old when her father died. One day he appeared to her, wrapt in fire. "My daughter," said he, "I will be plunged in fire till you have done penance for me." Then the child, with a rare courage, decided to practice the hardest mortifications, in order to pay the spiritual debts of her father. She succeeded. Her father appeared again, as bright as a Saint, saying: "God has accepted your suffrages and your satisfactory works, my daughter. 1 am going to enjoy eternal happiness. Do not cease to offer yourself as a victim for the salvation of Suffering Souls. This is the will of God."

Prayer: De Profundis

Let us pray for those who rest in the cemetery: O God, by whose mercy the Souls of the departed rest in peace, we beseech Thee to grant to Thy servants, and to all who rest in the Lord, the forgiveness of their sins, and life everlasting. Through our Lord Jesus Christ. Amen.

V. Eternal rest give unto them, O Lord.
R. And let perpetual light shine upon them.
V. May they rest in peace.
R. Amen.

The Ninth Day: Benefit of the Devotion to the "Poor Souls."

Say Preparatory Prayer

Meditation: This Novena is coming to a close. Do we understand the benefits and the consolation derived from devotion to the holy Souls? Do we need stronger motives to increase our zeal? Then let us consider that: Nothing is more glorious to God, nothing gives more honor to His Holy Name, nothing rejoices His Heart more, nothing is more pleasing to Him than charity for the "Poor Souls."

To open Heaven to the Poor Souls is to praise and glorify God, the number of hearts that love Him. "Such a work," says Bourdaloue, "is an apostolate more noble, more meritorious than the conversion of sinners, and even of heathens."

How we will please the Heart of Jesus, Who loves the Souls redeemed by His Precious Blood! He would willingly come into this world again and offer Himself for their deliverance; but all justice must be accomplished, and the debts of the Souls must be paid. Therefore, He has inspired His Church with the practice of praying for the dead every time the Holy Sacrifice is offered.

The Blessed Virgin is the Queen of Purgatory and will be highly gratified when we contribute to the relief of the "Poor Souls."

St. Joseph, the patron of a happy death, will also present our requests to the Lord, who has been called His Son. He will repay us generously if we come to the rescue of the suffering Souls.

What joy among the Saints in Heaven when they will see another elect---a Soul coming out of Purgatory! Her Guardian Angel, the Holy Patron, will welcome and congratulate her! It will be a great joy in Heaven. The Saints know the benefactors of the "Poor Souls," and they will, in return, protect them.

We have already said that the Saints in Purgatory will remember their benefactors. No, they cannot forget them! They will attentively provide for them in needs both temporal and spiritual. They will protect us and defend us in troubles, in dangers, in temptations. On our death-bed they will surround us. At the tribunal of God they will be our advocates; and, if we are cast into Purgatory, they will come to visit us, to console us, until the day of our entrance into a glorious eternity.

Practice: Give alms to the poor; insure your soul with prayers and good deeds against the fire of Purgatory. Money will be useless at the hour of death, but your good works will follow you.

Resolution: I will never miss the opportunity of assisting the "Poor Souls."

Example: A pious lady was praying for the recovery of her health. She had exhausted every means and made novenas after novenas to the Blessed Virgin Mary, to St. Joseph, etc., without success. But she was advised to commence novenas for the relief of the "Poor Souls" in Purgatory. She did so and entirely recovered. She was accustomed to say: "All that I ask through the intercession of the "Poor Souls" I obtain easily. With them I am never discouraged, and I hope against hope."

Prayer: De Profundis

Let us pray for all the faithful departed: O God, Creator and Redeemer of all men, we beseech Thee to grant to the Souls of Thy servants the remission of their sins, so that by our prayers they may obtain the indulgence for which they long. O Lord, Who reigns and lives, world without end. Amen.

V. Eternal rest give unto them, O Lord.
R. And let perpetual light shine upon them.
V. May they rest in peace.
R. Amen.

Christ the King Library
Delia Kansas

Printed in Great Britain
by Amazon.co.uk, Ltd.,
Marston Gate.